THE
BARBECUE
BOOK

Lamb and Peanut Burgers (page 50), Lamb and Kidney Kebabs (page 71)

THE
BARBECUE
BOOK

AUDREY ELLIS

Crescent Books

New York

ACKNOWLEDGMENTS

The author and publishers would like to thank the following companies for their help in supplying some of the photographs for this book:

Anchor Foods Limited (page 105)
British Alcan Consumer Products Limited (pages 87, 109)
British Bacon Bureau (pages 48, 51, 73)
British Chicken Information Service (page 46)
British Meat (pages 42, 53, 62, 70)
British Sausage Bureau (page 66)
British Trout Association Limited (page 37)
British Turkey Federation (pages 33, 112)
Butterball Foods (page 84)
Canned Food Advisory Service (page 118)
Cherry Valley Duckling (page 122)
Frank Odell Limited (pages 10, 15, 16, 17)
Hammonds of Yorkshire (pages 47, 55)
HJ Heinz Company Limited (page 90)
Hellmann's Real Mayonnaise (page 97)

Kellogg Company of Great Britain Limited (pages 49, 69, 93)
Kibun Limited (page 87)
KP Nuts (pages 77, 89)
Mushroom Grower's Association (page 65)
National Dairy Council (pages 101, 117)
New Zealand Lamb Information Bureau (pages 2, 6, 74)
Rayner Burgess Limited (pages 45, 56, 83)
Sarsons Limited (page 106)
Schwartz Spices (page 98)
Seafish Industry Authority (pages 79, 80)
JA Sharwood and Company Limited (page 121)
Summer Oranges (page 94)
THERMOS Gas Barbecues (pages 28, 31, 115)
Vision by Corning (page 125)
T Walls and Sons (page 35)
Whitworths Holdings Limited (page 67)

They also wish to acknowledge the assistance given in loaning barbecue equipment and accessories for photography by Frank Odell Limited of Teddington, Middlesex.

All remaining photography: John Lee

Illustrated by Michelle Illing
Jacket photography: Ian O'Leary
Food prepared for jacket photography: Jenny Schapter

Designed by Groom & Pickerill

First English edition published by
The Hamlyn Publishing Group Limited
Bridge House, Twickenham, Middlesex TW1 3SB, England

This 1987 edition published by Crescent Books
Distributed by Crown Publishers, Inc.
225 Park Avenue South
New York, New York 10003

ISBN 0–517–62952–6

h g f e d c b a

Printed in Italy

CONTENTS

Introduction 7

Useful Facts and Figures 9

Choosing Your Barbecue 11

Accessories and Tools 23

Cooking Methods 29

Foods to Barbecue 39

Introduction to Recipes 41

Broiling 43

Skewer and Kebab Cooking 63

Spit-Roasting and Parcel Cooking 81

Salads and Sauces 91

Extra Delights 103

Barbecue Menus for Guests 113

Index 128

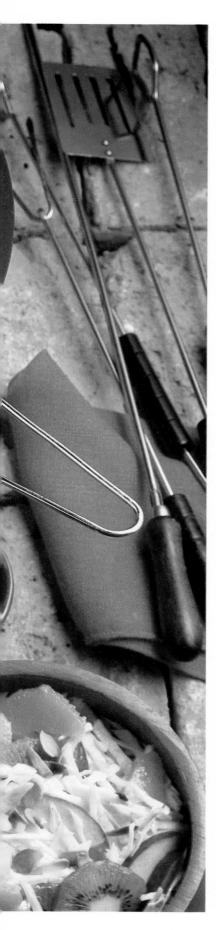

INTRODUCTION

Which remote ancestor of ours first discovered that raw meat tasted better when cooked over an open fire – primarily designed to prevent attacks by dangerous animals and keep his family warm during chilly nights? No one can say, or why it is that the tantalizing aroma and taste of food cooked by this age-old method appeals so strongly today. The fact is that this simple form of cooking has become part of our lives again, in preference, weather permitting, to quick-and-easy food preparation in even the most modern of kitchens.

There are excellent reasons, quite apart from the food itself tasting so good. Barbecuing is fun, it is a group activity, a friendly affair. Maybe just for yourselves, or to entertain guests; everyone wants to take an active part. Perhaps encouraged by holidays abroad, neither the primmest among us nor the most serious-minded feels awkward about donning an apron and heatproof mitts and taking the helm at a barbecue party. Don't be shy about producing your special barbecue sauces, tips for tenderizing cheaper cuts of meat, and your cunning methods of encouraging a sulky fire to provide a glowing bed of coals, ready for the first items to slide on the grid. The other eager participants really enjoy watching the preparations, and smelling the delicious odor as the food sizzles and browns.

It doesn't even cost much. Certainly an excellent and ample meal can be provided at far less than one would pay in a restaurant. Children, of course, adore the really simple items. Sausage links of the fresh pork or smoked varieties, hamburgers to put inside buns slathered with relish, keep them happy.

For a big gathering, enthusiasts will help out by bringing their own portable barbecues, so masses of food can be prepared at the same time. And just in case some of the party are vegetarians, or wedded to the low-salt diet, I have included some special recipes for them.

To finish the meal with style, there are butterscotch and chocolate fondue dips, toasted marshmallows, fruit salads, both hot and cold.

If you remember boy scout days, bring bananas and raw sausages. Strip the skins carefully off the bananas, eat them to keep hunger pangs at bay, enclose the sausages in the empty skins, and put them over the fire or into the ashes to cook. It's informal, but that's the essential spirit of barbecue cooking.

To learn a great deal more about how to choose, use and produce superb results with your barbecue, read on. Then take your pick from a host of mouthwatering recipes.

Butterflied Leg of Lamb (page 57), Lamb Steaks with Fruit Side Dish (page 85), Wellington Lamb Kebabs (page 74)

Audrey Ellis

USEFUL FACTS AND FIGURES

Measuring accurately

Correct measuring of ingredients is essential to ensure consistent results. All measurements given in this book are level unless otherwise stated.

Choosing measuring cups: When purchasing measuring cups you should choose one set for dry ingredients and another for liquids.

For dry ingredients: Buy a set of four graduated measuring cups consisting of a $\frac{1}{4}$-cup, $\frac{1}{3}$-cup, $\frac{1}{2}$-cup and 1-cup measure. Always level off with the edge of a spatula or knife.

For liquid ingredients: Buy a 1-cup measuring cup, the rim of which is above the 1-cup line to avoid spillage. 2-cup and 1-quart size measuring cups are also very useful. Set the cup on a level surface. Lower your head so that the measuring line will be at eye level and fill the cup up to the correct mark.

Choosing measuring spoons: A good set of measuring spoons will give you accurate small measurements. It should include $\frac{1}{8}$-teaspoon, $\frac{1}{4}$-teaspoon, $\frac{1}{2}$-teaspoon, 1-teaspoon, $\frac{1}{2}$-tablespoon and 1-tablespoon measurements. 16 tablespoons equal 1 cup.

Equivalent measures

3 teaspoons	1 tablespoon
2 tablespoons	$\frac{1}{8}$ cup
4 tablespoons	$\frac{1}{4}$ cup
5 tablespoons + 1 teaspoon	$\frac{1}{3}$ cup
8 tablespoons	$\frac{1}{2}$ cup
10 tablespoons + 2 teaspoons	$\frac{2}{3}$ cup
12 tablespoons	$\frac{3}{4}$ cup
16 tablespoons	1 cup
2 cups	1 pint
2 pints	1 quart
1 quart	4 cups
4 quarts	1 gallon
16 oz. (dry measure)	1 lb.

Equivalents

Butter or margarine

2 tablespoons	1 oz.
$\frac{1}{2}$ cup	$\frac{1}{4}$ lb. (one stick)
2 cups	1 lb.

Dairy products

1 cup cream	2 cups whipped cream
1 cup cottage cheese	8 oz.
$\frac{1}{4}$ lb. Cheddar or American cheese	1 cup shredded or grated

Flour

Flour is sifted before measuring

4 cups all-purpose flour	1 lb.
2 tablespoons flour	1 tablespoon cornstarch for thickening
5 teaspoons flour	2 teaspoons arrowroot for thickening

Sugar

Confectioner's sugar is measured before sifting
Brown sugar is measured firmly packed

2 cups sugar	1 lb.
$3\frac{1}{4}$ cups confectioner's sugar	1 lb.
$2\frac{1}{4}$ cups brown sugar	1 lb.

Miscellaneous

1 orange	about 8 tablespoons juice
1 lemon or lime	2–3 tablespoons juice
Grated rind of one orange	about 1 tablespoon
Grated rind of one lemon	$1\frac{1}{2}$–2 teaspoons
1 lb. nuts in the shell	about 2 cups nut meats
$\frac{1}{4}$ lb. chopped nuts	scant 1 cup
1 lb. seedless raisins	about 3 cups
1 square chocolate unsweetened or semisweet	1 oz.
1 cup honey	$1\frac{1}{4}$ cups sugar + $\frac{1}{4}$ cup liquid

Barbecued Steak, Salmon and Chicken Drumsticks.
Baked Potatoes with Garlic and Herb Butter (page 104).

CHOOSING YOUR BARBECUE

The very idea of barbecue cooking instantly spurs one's imagination to form delightful pictures of eating in the open air, in perfect weather with just a hint of smoke about to sharpen healthy appetites. The reality may fall a little short of the rosy picture most people conjure up, when they discover that food takes quite a while to cook when the fire is sulky, and their eyes stream because smoke from burning fat isn't always agreeable. But if you're not deterred by such set-backs, and find that the first time you go to a barbecue it's a thrilling experience, quite likely you'll want to make, buy or even build a barbecue yourself and can hardly wait to give your own party.

Fortunately you need not spend a fortune only to find that barbecuing is not the hobby for you after all. It's no great expense to start in a small way with an improvised grill and a bag of charcoal. Then, if you've well and truly caught the barbecuing bug, decide whether it will suit you best to improvise, build a permanent structure or invest in a manufactured barbecue. There's a great range on the market for you to choose from.

Improvised Grills

A large earthenware flowerpot, not of course a plastic one, can be used as a container for charcoal. Raise the pot on at least two courses of bricks to bring it to a comfortable height and to increase the draft which can only enter through the central hole in the bottom of the pot. Some air spaces between the bricks themselves are essential. An old metal oven shelf or refrigerator rack can serve as a grid.

It is not so easy as it used to be to find a large square cookie tin or deep roasting pan which you can pension off to make a barbecue. If you have such an item, punch holes in the sides near the base to make air vents. Again, it would be better to raise this on two courses of bricks so that you do not have to bend double every time you want to place food on the grid. It is worthwhile to approach a local builders' merchant to see whether he can supply a few fire bricks cheaply, since these specially hardened bricks are quite expensive. A

Party Grill Super Wagon

gravel drive is a very good and safe base for a barbecue, if it continues round the side of the house, out of sight of passers-by. If there is no oven or refrigerator grid available, chicken wire folded double or treble thickness would serve. Only make sure to tuck in loose ends of wire firmly with a pair of pliers so that no one will catch their fingers.

Another improvisation which is extremely mobile can be effected by using an old metal wheelbarrow. Often, these are rusty with the beginnings of a hole in the bottom. Make sure the charcoal fire will not suddenly fall through, although it is a good precaution always to place the wheelbarrow on a paved or gravelled area. The front wheel can be raised on bricks or pieces of paving to get the firebed level. Lay a line of bricks along each side in the barrow to contain the fire and provide a support for the grid. Although you can wheel the barrow about to find a good site, remember that it is unwise to move it while the barbecue is alight.

Try various positions for your barbecue on the patio or in a sheltered part of the garden where there is no foliage to catch fire. This is a great advantage when you decide to build a permanent structure because you need to know how the fire will react to the prevailing wind and under different wind conditions. Sometimes an attractive looking situation fills the surrounding area with smoke, or does not provide a good draft to get the fire going. Usually a walled patio gives you ready-made backing for the grill and is the first choice providing it isn't too close to the house.

Movable wheelbarrow barbecue

Campfire-style barbecuing

For real barbecue enthusiasts, nothing is more fun than to set out with food supplies, a bag of fuel, some firelighters, matches and a cooking grid. Your destination will decide whether you need to take other essentials, but the kind of terrain you are looking for should be one with a plentiful supply of rocks, stones or pebbles. A wooded area with clearings usually provides one large rock on which to build the fire and large stones which you can place on three sides, leaving the front open to encourage a lively glow. Set your grid firmly on the stones, if necessary using smaller ones to create a level surface, then another border of stones around the edge of the grid to hold it firmly. Take no risk that the grid may slip and allow its precious load of food to fall into the fire.

Seasonal brick structure

Improvised grill

If you are taking a trip to the sea, the beach you choose may be flat and sandy with occasional outcrops of rock. This sometimes provides a perfect site for your barbecue created by nature. Pebbly beaches, although safe from the danger of the fire spreading, are usually sloping ones. Find the flattest area where you can use the larger pebbles rather as you would bricks for building purposes.

Of course you should always dismantle these temporary barbecues before you go home, making sure that all traces of fire are completely extinguished and that no unsightly evidence of your visit is left behind.

Seasonal structures

Many enthusiasts are quite happy to settle for a semi-permanent structure, shaped like a square chimney or like a round well. It is built up with layers of unmortared bricks in the same way as a child builds with wooden or plastic blocks, and leaving small apertures between the bricks. In a round construction the spaces are wedge shaped. These structures are quite sturdy as the open join comes always in the center of the bricks above and below it. The whole edifice can be dismantled when the cold weather sets in and the bricks stored for next season. You can buy round, square or rectangular racks for holding the fire and the food from most barbecue stockists and you will need about one hundred bricks. To make a good job at the lowest cost, try to acquire some over-burnt house bricks; that is bricks of good quality that have been left too long in the kiln. They are very hard and less likely to crack than ordinary house bricks.

Built-in Barbecues

Once you are truly convinced that you need to build a barbecue into your lifestyle, rather than improvise, or dismantle it every winter, consider the design very carefully. You can buy a do-it-yourself kit with the basic components: a baseplate to collect the ash, a strong fire grate for the charcoal and a grid for the food. Ideally, you should build in supports at several levels for the grill so that it can be raised or lowered according to the heat you require.

The suggested designs shown here are for a very simple barbecue and for something more elaborate, which includes fitted doors below the grate to allow easy removal of the ashes. Remember that if you intend buying a rotisserie unit, containing the spit, support brackets, meat clamps and motor operated by battery, it will protrude at either side of the top surface.

Although it is very handy to have a long work surface adjacent to the fire grate, it takes considerable space. Below the work surface is an ideal situation to store your barbecue tools and perhaps underneath that, built-in storage space for supplies of charcoal, briquets, or wood chips. It all depends how much garden or patio space you are willing to sacrifice to your barbecue.

Other refinements which are not beyond the capabilities of an amateur enthusiast are the installation of a sink with water on tap and an outdoor light. This latter item can be rigged up by an overhead cable but if you insist on an underground cable, consult a qualified electrician.

Firm foundations

A permanent installation may be quite heavy and will require a proper foundation. If your chosen site is a patio, you can assume that it will be both level and stable (although it is always worthwhile checking with a spirit level that the top of the barbecue is perfectly level). If it is not to be erected on a patio, but directly on the earth, make sure that the soil is well compacted. If it has been dug over at some time in the past, possibly for flower or vegetable beds, there may be a certain amount of subsidence and that would not really be a good area to choose. Assuming that the site has not been disturbed for at least five years previously, you need only excavate about 8 inches before filling in with hardcore and a 2-inch layer of cement, damp sand and gravel. A do-it-yourself consultant will advise you on the proportions to use.

As the area round the barbecue tends to get churned up by eager helpers, it is best to surround it with some sort of paving. All kinds of paving slabs, which much reduce the risk of slipping, are available to choose from; some in very attractive soft shades of honey, blue, green and others. Many enterprising manufacturers of building materials sell kits of reconstituted stone blocks for this purpose, including some wider blocks to be used as supports.

Built-in barbecue

Manufactured Barbecues

Probably the best advice one can give is – start small. It would be a pity to lash out on a big wagon and then find that you still preferred using your home-built brick grill.

Open braziers

The simplest model of this kind has three tubular legs which bolt on, clip or screw in, and a windshield which slots very easily into place. It is particularly suitable to transport for picnics as it takes up very little room in the back of the car, but the firebowl ($13\frac{1}{2}$ inches in diameter) does not permit many items to be cooked at the same time. A more elaborate picnic model has a higher windshield, a slightly larger firebowl and a useful undershelf. Another alternative has two wheels and a handle to make it completely mobile, and a wire rack instead of the undershelf which holds the three-legged frame rigid when you are wheeling it about. Even these small braziers can accommodate rotisserie units, which can be set at different levels above the firebowl.

Larger sized braziers range up to 26 inches in diameter. These larger models often have two wooden handles on the food grill so that it can be lifted and positioned at any height you wish above the fire, using slots in the windshield.

Open brazier

Hooded braziers

Even a deeper windshield is not always proof against gusty winds. The hooded brazier provides the perfect answer. The half-hood clamps on the edge of the firebowl and serves three important functions. It conserves heat over the food cooking on the grid; it prevents smoke from blowing about in every direction; and it gives a really firm support for a rotisserie unit. A revolving grill can be adjusted in height by means of a crank handle situated beneath the firebowl, or by spinning the grill on a threaded shaft.

Although some hooded barbecues include a warming compartment, they are difficult to find, but plates can be placed on top of the hood which naturally becomes hot during cooking.

Kettle barbecues

Cooking with a kettle barbecue is much more like conventional oven cooking. By adjusting vents in the hood and bowl, you can control the circulation of air through the fire and therefore the temperature. Even a large turkey or joint of meat can be cooked as perfectly as in your electric oven in the kitchen. Instead of being dissipated, heat is conserved and reflected back on to the food from all the surfaces, even the inside of the cover. Turning is therefore rarely necessary and basting reduced to a minimum. When the hood is on, there are no flames to cause flare-ups. So it is easy to keep clean.

Cooking temperature can be lowered by closing the dampers a little or raised by opening them to let in more air. Not only can you use this facility to control the draft required to get the fire going but, when you have finished cooking, the fire can quickly be extinguished by closing them completely; cutting off the air supply. These features reduce the amount of fuel consumed and therefore the running cost is comparatively low. Unburnt charcoal remains ready to light up quickly next time.

Although keen barbecuers are by nature optimistic, the closed kettle performs better than any other in bad weather, which makes the original investment worthwhile. These barbecues are constructed very sturdily, which means that they are costly. One reason is that the lid must fit closely and not become distorted – always a danger when overenthusiastic guests are rather rough with your equipment. Both hood and firebowl are made from steel, very resistant to distortion. They are covered inside and out with porcelain enamel. This strong finish prevents rust, corrosion and stains.

Left: Good Time Super Fiesta. Right: Big Time Hooded Grill

Round kettles
Both bowls and domes are fitted with handles (since you would certainly burn yourself if you tried to remove the hood without them). Some models have an ash pan fitted inside the base of the bowl, which prevents ash dropping through being spread about by every breeze. Rather more models have a dished pan into which the ash falls, which simply slots into the three legs and locks on turning. This can be very easily removed to empty out the ashes.

Square kettles with hinged hoods
Many barbecue cooks prefer the hinged rather than lift-off lid. When open, the hood acts as a wind-shield and another advantage of the square shape is that it is so convenient to attach side tables to provide working and warming space.

A square grid provides at least 20 per cent more cooking surface than a round one, which is important if you frequently cook for a crowd. Although the basic hooded grill simply stands on four sturdy tubular legs, other models are provided with a strut and two wheels so that the barbecue can be easily moved and stands very firmly. An extra refinement has been introduced – instead of three separately controlled air vents, there is a lever which adjusts all three vents simultaneously and, at the same time, acts as a riddler to shake out the ash.

Wagons
New ideas constantly emerge and one of the latest and most interesting is the Groovy Grill, a wagon without wheels. The food is arranged on a grooved, sloping grill plate so that the fatty juices run down into a collecting tray instead of dropping through the bars of a grid on to the fire. This achieves two objects – virtually fat-free cooking which is impor-tant to those on a low-fat diet, and minimal flare-ups. If you barbecue in your garden, your neighbors will undoubtedly appreciate this benefit!

You yourself will be glad that the grill plate is porcelain enamelled for easy cleaning and has such strong handles. The fat in the collecting tray can easily be poured off. The firebox can be placed at

Double and Triple Hibachis

various levels to raise or lower the cooking heat. You can also adjust the angle slightly, since it is deep enough to do this safely, lifting it up or down by means of two "ladder" pieces on either side. The ladder rungs can be located in different slots in the frame to give varying angles. There is a useful lower shelf.

More traditional wagon barbecues have wheels so that they can be moved about quite conveniently. The most useful type has a removable firebowl set into a robust two-wheeled trolley, with a hinged hood. The open hood acts as a windshield; it can be closed for covered cooking, or fitted with a spit rod to be used as a rotisserie. There is lots of room at the side of the cooking area for stacking plates and a solid lower shelf. (A simpler type of wagon has a round brazier firebowl and windshield mounted in a wagon.)

The wagon chassis is rectangular with either two or four wheels and comes in a variety of materials such as cast iron or aluminum, sheet metal and hardwood. The cost is very much influenced by the weight and stability of the material used. It is the choice of those people who require similar facilities to a built-in barbecue, yet be able to move it about. Extras the more expensive models might include are gauges for measuring cooking temperature, warming areas and fully motorized spits. In one model, the fire can be held

vertically to produce a wall of heat for spit-roasting. This sounds as though it might be unsafe but in fact the food grill can be located in slots in the sides to hold it vertically, and the fuel is put in behind this. Food on the spit drips into a tray placed in the empty firebox.

Hibachis
The hibachi has the great advantage of being so easily portable and yet being very strongly constructed from cast iron, with the latest models being all-steel versions. Hibachi is not a trade name but the Japanese word for a small heater. Originally all hibachis were solid cast iron fireboxes fitted with grills. They are rectangular in shape and draft vents in the base make it easy to light the fire and control the cooking heat. If there is a handy ladder-rack at the back, the cooking grids, fitted with shaped wooden handles, can be set at three different levels. The latest models have wooden feet, with tubular metal spacers to separate them from the firebox, for stability and safety.

Hibachis are reasonably cheap so it is worth buying a double or triple size. If occasionally you are only intending to barbecue a small quantity of food, you need only light a fire under one of the cooking grids.

16

Pack-away portables

The latest word in portables is the mini barbecue which comes complete in a stylish carrying case. Only a little larger than a document case is the Grill Box which, when you open it up, contains an ash box, two detachable metal brackets to support it, and a rectangular plated grill with its own handle, which can be slotted in to adjust the cooking level. It would cope adequately with four chicken portions or large chops, plus a few tomatoes, but obviously the cooking space is severely limited.

Gas barbecues

If you are prepared to use bottled gas, which is now readily available, you may prefer to forget all about the mess and fuss of using solid fuel. Although many people feel that they lose something of the pioneer spirit in abandoning the challenge of getting a good fire going, gas is cleaner, quicker and truly convenient. Most gas barbecues are provided with automatic ignition and the heat can be controlled almost by the touch of a fingertip. If your unit does not light automatically, all you need

Portable Grill Box

to do is insert a match through the hole provided. Within 15 minutes the lava rock, with which the barbecue is equipped, will be hot enough to start cooking. You won't miss any of the true outdoor-cooked flavor, because this actually comes from smoke created by fat and juices from the food as it cooks, dripping on to the hot rocks.

The color of the gas cylinders is important. Propane gas is supplied in cylinders painted red or orange and has one great advantage over Butane gas which is supplied in cylinders painted white. Propane has a lower freezing temperature and could be used even in very cold weather, if you are such an enthusiast that you want to barbecue even in winter. But for domestic use, Butane gas is usually supplied. (It is most unusual, by the way, to link up your barbecue to the main gas supply.) Always connect a cylinder with care and keep Butane cylinders upright. Portables use Propane cartridges which are disposable after use, and the cylinder may be tilted.

Because they are not consumed as charcoal briquets are, the lava rocks absorb grease as a sponge soaks up water. There are various methods to clean them. One is to boil the rocks in just

sufficient water to cover them, with a few drops of detergent added. Make sure the rocks dry out thoroughly before re-use. Some people think the flavor of food is not so appetizing afterwards. Another method is to clean the rocks when the barbecue session is over. Keep the barbecue lid closed over the rocks while you subject them to high heat for about 10 minutes by turning the barbecue up. These processes may sound troublesome, but after all there is no ash to be removed or bags of fuel to be transported.

There are three types of gas barbecue, the portable, the pedestal and the wagon, all with hinged hoods.

Portable Gas Barbecues

Although heavy for its size, this model is very easy to transport. It has folding legs and a small disposable Propane cartridge – the whole works would fit easily into the back of a car, along with picnic tables and chairs.

Pedestal Gas Barbecues

Although one may miss the handy side tables and extra storage space of the wagon on a basic model, a pedestal gas barbecue is less costly and takes up little space on a small patio. Wheels and a metal transport handle allow the barbecue to be moved about. You can always attach side shelves later since they are available accessories. Some models have a two-piece two-position cooking grid with twin burners which can be individually controlled. This enables you to cook a wider range of food than is possible with the basic cooking grid. A separate baking rack increases the cooking area, even if it is only used to warm rolls or keep cooked food hot.

Gas Wagons

These elaborate and expensive pieces of equipment permit you to cook even a large joint on the rotisserie, grill several types of food at different cooking levels and feature variable position lids. You'll get a big control panel for your money, storage drawers and one side table if not two.

Gas Barbecue Safety Tips

There are a few special safety tips for users of gas barbecues which are dictated by common sense.
- Have your match or other means of lighting ready before you turn on the fuel supply. Also make sure that the lid of the barbecue is open.
- When you change a cylinder, make sure first that the barbecue is switched off and completely cold.
- Use a torch if your sense of smell suggests to you that the gas is leaking. Never a naked flame, of course!

Electric barbecues

Yes, you can even get an electric barbecue, provided there is a suitable socket to plug it in where you want to cook: perhaps where you would plug in your electric lawn mower, for they come supplied with 32 feet of cable.

Universal barbecues

This type of barbecue has a basic unit in the shape of a triangular column. It has four brackets on each side, on which to hook food grills at various heights above the heat. The fire is contained in three wedge-shaped bowls, fitting together to form a circle. You may use one firebowl only, two or all three. This gives you a great variation of choices on how to cook the food. One fire may be made hotter by crowding the briquets together, while another section is used for slow cooking. The height at which you attach the various grids also influences the speed of cooking.

Getting Back to Nature

Al fresco cooking need not depend on bought barbecue appliances at all. You can, if the law permits, build a fire of wood, using the age-old principles. It does carry a great responsibility; forgetting to put the fire out *completely* could put an entire woodland area at risk after your departure. But if you decide to try it out, dig a narrow trench, or just scrape it out with a sharp and stout knife, around the fire area. Tree roots have been known to catch fire and smolder, unnoticed, for days, and then burst into flame yards away from the site of the original campfire. Even sparks flying to land on plants or shrubs in a thicket at some distance can be dangerous long after you've left the scene.

Having taken these precautions, here's how to start the fun. Begin by collecting dead branches and stripping them of twigs. Whether your fire base is a flat rock, or just a patch of hard earth, pile up the branches *loosely* using the small twigs first, with perhaps an encouraging ball of crumpled newspaper at the heart. Thrust in a lighted match and, as the tiny twigs blaze up, add larger ones, then the branches, always adding fuel on the downwind side. Since air is as important as the fuel itself, let the fire breathe, don't tamp down the twigs hoping the larger ones will catch fire more quickly.

Smoke is troublesome, and there is bound to be some, but hardwoods smoke less, besides provid-

ing more heat than softwoods. Oak, beech and ash are best, then the wood from evergreens such as pine. Beechwood is not recommended, as it sizzles and spits in burning. Don't let the fire get larger in circumference, keep it neat and small, to intensify the heat as well as for safety.

Few people would be unwise enough to leave an open fire untended, or within any proximity to overhanging branches, or be without a water spray of some sort for dousing. But if you're full of campfire enthusiasm, use the old Indian methods of putting it out. Scoop up a shovelful of damp mud, or make it by mixing loose soil with water, and pour it over. Damp sand works equally well.

Another good tip is to remember that wood fires, unlike charcoal, create a lot of soot on the bottom of your pans. Film over the base of each pan with soap or liquid detergent before putting it over the flames. It will not prevent soot from forming, but makes it easy to remove.

Pit-cooking

This term conjures up visions of a Hawaiian luau, the roasting of whole pigs, and the like. But your pit may be a small hole, designed just to accommodate a big earthenware or metal bean pot, or soup pot, and the kind of covered roaster, maybe with a dimpled lid, which can be inverted, and used as a receptacle for more hot embers, to cook the food in the roaster from above as well as below. Put embers from your fire into the pit, cover with old grids, a few inches above them, and stand your pots on the grids. Make sure that all the cooking utensils are well below the top of the pit. Cover it with old planks, then with a tarpaulin sheet. Weight down the edges with bricks or stones.

Fuel and Fire-making

Charcoal is obtained by burning wood excluding oxygen, so that it carbonizes instead of burning with a flame. This produces a smokeless fuel which gives out a far greater and cleaner heat than untreated wood or coal. It reduces to nothing but a fine ash, and is therefore the ideal fuel for the barbecue.

Charcoal

Charcoal-burning used to be a skilled craft, carried out in a forest glade, transforming masses of timber into a convenient compressed fuel; and although it is now factory produced, the finished result can vary very much in quality. If you fail to get the fire started without a great deal of trouble, or feel that the charcoal soon burns out, try another brand. Really good charcoal lights promptly, provides consistent high heat and even if relatively expensive, burns longer than a cheaper product. Don't judge the price of the bag by its size. The best quality is made from hardwoods but some softwoods may be added. As charcoal emerges from the kiln in lumps which are too large for a barbecue, the lumps are broken up into pieces of a smaller, uniform size. When you empty the bag, there should be hardly any dust and tiny fragments at the bottom.

Charcoal briquets

It is more usual to buy briquets, formed into pillow or rod-shaped pieces. There may be additives to produce a fuel which burns for twice as long as pure hardwood charcoal, making briquets considerably cheaper to use. The best quality briquets are basically manufactured from hardwoods, which have a low resin content, because sparks tend to fly out if only a very small amount of high-resin softwood is incorporated.

Instant lighting fuels are not cheap but ideal when speed and convenience matter most, possibly for a small meal that has to be prepared quickly. For a big family barbecue, and if entertaining a crowd, hardwood charcoal or briquets are preferable.

Firelighters

A briquet has a very high density and is therefore not as easy to ignite as a piece of charcoal. Fortunately there are all kinds of starters to make lighting easier. All are intended to be used before the fire is lit and should never be added later.

Although solid firelighters are the most popular, suppliers usually stock a fluid lighter; lighter sachets, which are clean, odorless and my personal preference – there is even a lighter paste. Instructions are given on the container and, if carefully followed, ensure very quick ignition.

If you want to try the latest trick of the trade, there is an instant burning charcoal which promises you the capability of actually starting to cook within 15 minutes – ideal for the impatient barbecue chef. A similar product is sold in bags, which is very clean to handle and doesn't require lighting agents either.

If your problem is not so much lighting the fire but ensuring that it cooks efficiently, you might like to try a charcoal underbase. It is a gritty-looking substance resembling gravel, which should be spread in the base of the firebowl before you build the fire. It certainly protects and prolongs the life of the firebowl and is intended to give good air circulation through the fuel, absorb excessive grease and thus reduce those irritating flare-ups.

Now that milk and cream are so often packaged in waxed cartons, you may find a use for them as free firelighters. Tear up some newspaper almost as fine as confetti, and pack into a dry waxed carton with a few briquets. Sink this into the pile of briquets and apply a match to it. Hey presto! (But don't try this trick with plastic cartons, as it does not work.)

Shaping your fire

Some amount of control over the heat of your fire can be obtained by the way you arrange the coals. Intense direct heat comes from an even bed of coals spread under the grilling area and extending beyond it a little all round. If the fire gets too hot, you can cool it down by spreading out the coals, allowing some air to come up through the spaces between them. This soon cools them, but if too much, push them together again, shaking out any build-up of ash, and add a few more briquets.

Dividing the coals – a metal drip pan may be placed under the grid, centered, with an equal amount of coals on either side. Put the grid over this and place food, which may drip fat on to the coals and cause a flare-up, directly above the pan.

The simplest way to vary heat is not by shaping the fire but by moving the grill grid up, and away from the source of heat, to cook more slowly; or by moving it down and closer to the fire to cook more quickly. If no adjustment is possible, move the food you wish to cook more slowly out to the sides of the grill, since the hottest part is always in the center.

When to start cooking

It may take up to 40 minutes for your fire to reach a high heat. Personally, I believe the golden rule is to leave the coals alone and not rake them about to encourage them. A gas barbecue has the great advantage that it needs only 15 minutes to reach a comparable heat and is even more flexible if you choose a unit with adjustable controls.

Extinguishing the fire

Charcoal has the great virtue of continuing to burn until nothing remains but a fine ash. But this is rather a waste if you have finished cooking and plenty of unburnt charcoal is visible. As has already been explained, closing the dampers on covered barbecues excludes oxygen and puts out the fire.

On other types, you can carefully transfer hot coals, using an old shovel or preferably a pair of large tongs, to a metal bucket with a lid. Closing the lid has the same effect. If there is no lid, shovel or lift the coals, a few at a time, into a metal pail containing some water, using great care to avoid the steam which will immediately rise into the air. Later, drain off the water and leave the coals to dry out thoroughly before re-use.

Safety first

A barbecue is, by its very nature, accident prone like any other open fire. Certain rules should never be broken.

It is unsafe to encourage the fire by adding a sprinkling of lighter fluid or any volatile fuel. Even if this were not a dangerous practice, it gives a nasty taste like kerosene to the food. Check that a liquid starter, if you use one, is a product intended for charcoal. Other volatile substances may actually explode, causing a shock at the best, nasty burns at worst. *It is unwise to pour any form of liquid starter on hot coals* – a point that cannot be over-emphasized. Sometimes these appear to have been quenched, but they might suddenly flare up. It is far better to use bellows or a barbecue fan.

Some families choose only to use the starter as a pre-soak treatment for a few briquets. Just soak about half a dozen in a jar filled with the starter. Place these treated briquets on the base of the firebed, then cover with ordinary ones from the bag before lighting. This certainly is a very safe method.

Once the fire is going, keep a watchful eye on all members of the party, especially children. Bring along a bag of old, dilapidated pairs of tough gloves, and make sure everyone wears gloves before approaching the fire. Train members of the family always to contribute discarded gloves to the barbecue bag! Show the assembled company the water spray for dousing flare-ups (children will love to use a water-pistol). Point out where it's kept.

Most of my readers will smile at the idea of barbecuing indoors, for it's so essentially an outdoor sport. If a change from good to bad weather tempts you to move inside, any equipment that is charcoal-fired must be placed in a fireplace where carbon monoxide fumes can be carried off completely up the chimney. Even the entrance to a garage, or some other sort of outbuilding made of brick with open doors, is not recommended. If the wind blows the fumes *into* the garage, they can be dangerous.

Water pistol to extinguish fire

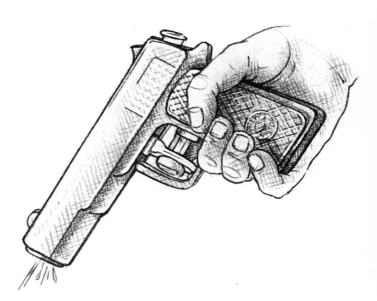

Storing your equipment

The metal parts of a permanent or improvised barbecue will probably come to no harm if left out all summer. But when you decide that the barbecue season is over for the year, clean them all thoroughly and cover with a thin film of vegetable oil before wrapping and putting away. Paper is fine for wrapping, but try to put all the parts together in a plastic bag, well sealed to keep them safe from damp and attack by rust.

ACCESSORIES AND TOOLS

Just buying a barbecue, or building one in your garden, is not the end of the story. Even if you are not intending to cook anything elaborate, you will need fuel and a great many special tools not always to be found in the kitchen.

Assuming that you will start in a modest fashion, here's a list of items you will need, apart from other more sophisticated ones you may like to add to your collection when you can afford them: Lighting fluid or kindling, charcoal, charcoal briquets or wood chips; poker to level off fire; bellows to help light it; matches securely packed in a glass jar with screw top, so that they are visible but cannot accidentally catch fire; bib-type apron; rolls of paper towels or package of paper napkins; padded holders and gloves with heatproof palms (preferably those which come up over the wrist); tongs for turning food; small, strong, even if somewhat battered pans for sauces; brushes for applying sauces; sharp, sturdy carving knives and appropriate forks.

Optional items you would find useful: Long-handled hinged wire grid with close mesh; platters to hold cooked items that could be placed on the barbecue for a few minutes (stainless steel relegated from dining-room use, for instance); barbecue trays disposable after a few uses, or doubled chicken wire, holes spaced to give a narrow grid. These last are especially useful when barbecuing foods that tend to blacken and leave a strong-smelling residue on the grid, so that cleaning is a tiresome task.

Extra Tools and Accessories

Here are some of the aids to better barbecuing you may choose to invest in:

Tool sets
Don't make the mistake of thinking that every tool set includes the same selection. For instance, some have tongs, others do not. Compare several boxes (for this is the most economical way to buy them) before you choose. You can decide on those which seem the right length for you to handle conveniently and safely, and include the most useful selection, then perhaps buy the tongs separately. Scissor tongs are easier to manipulate than pincer

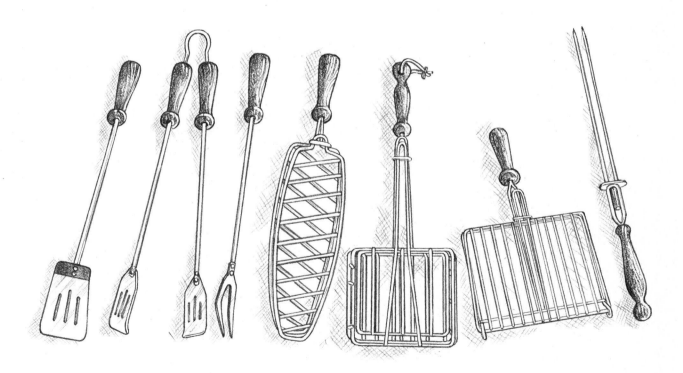

Barbecue Rump Steak and Baked Potatoes with Seasoned Sour Cream and Chives (page 107)

23

tongs if your wrist is not particularly strong. Remember that wooden handles do occasionally come over the heat and burn, or at least char slightly. Some tools I like more, have very strong red plastic handles, which never flare up, nor do they melt if quickly retrieved from the fire. They are also easy to clean and the handles look as good as new after many uses. If you want to be able to hang up the tools, and many barbecues have hooks to accommodate them, go for the type with fairly large holes in the handles, or thongs threaded through small holes, on which they can dangle.

Spit rod

Make sure when you buy this as an extra accessory that it will fit your particular barbecue. They are usually 24 inches overall length, and include a handle and meat forks or clamps which can be moved along the skewer to exactly the position where you wish to insert them in the meat, and then screwed tight. A battery-driven spit motor is really a 'must', but as they are sold without the battery, make sure you buy the right size battery. Turning by hand is a tiresome business for which you will not find many willing volunteers.

Bulb baster

Some bastes are easier to apply with this syringe-type tool, than with a brush. Draw up juices from a pan resting on the grid, if it is deep enough, or from a jug of the baste, and squirt over the food to be basted. The rubber section you squeeze must be gently detached from the plastic tube for cleaning, otherwise stale fat will accumulate inside it and go rancid.

Wire broilers

These come in single or triple fish-shaped holders, or steak/chop holders. There are also deep vegetable baskets. The food is inserted between the two halves of the hinged frame and a small clip is pushed down the handle to hold the frame securely closed. This makes turning the food, several times if necessary, quite simple.

Making an improvised brazier hood

You will need some 22 gauge galvanized steel wire. Form a ring exactly the diameter and circumference of the firebowl, overlapping by 2 inches and securing the overlap firmly with a piece of thinner wire. Check that the circle is a perfect fit. Make 3 or 4 half-hoops from the thick wire, allowing sufficient extra length to wrap the ends several times round the original circle. Shape and secure with pliers. Use more thin wire to secure them at the point where they all cross on top. Check again that the hood is a good fit. Cover the frame by smoothing on sheets of heavy-duty foil, dull side outwards, crimping the seams firmly. Make 2 small holes near the top of the hood to allow smoke to escape. Always use oven gloves to move the hood as it will be very hot. Re-cover with fresh foil whenever necessary.

Hickory chips

To give an authentic smokey taste to barbecued food, soak some hickory chips in water and sprinkle them on the fire during the cooking time.

Garden flares

To make your evening barbecues more enjoyable, illuminate the scene with these flares, molded round bamboo stakes which you can stick into the lawn. They can equally well be placed in flower beds or tubs of earth. Garden flares come in various attractive colors and shapes, and burn for up to two hours, usually long enough for a firelight party.

Beach Barbecued Red Mullet (page 59)

Citronella candles

Stinging winged insects are not deterred from attack by light alone, and are sometimes active even in the dark. Wax candles impregnated with oil of citronella give a soft romantic glow to the scene and scare off these unwelcome guests. The candles come in pretty holders of various colors, burn from 40–70 hours, so will serve for many an evening barbecue.

Wooden skewers

For small kebabs these skewers are disposable but will sometimes last for three or four uses if carefully cleaned. You will see from the pack that they should be soaked in water before use to prevent them from burning. This is not essential if the food is packed closely together, but it is certainly wiser to soak the ends as they will otherwise char quickly.

Barbecue grill trays

These really strong aluminum foil trays are shaped with runnels to collect fats dripping from the food being cooked in the tray, and yet allow charcoal smoke to pass through small vents and flavor the food. Pieces of food cannot slip through, as they might through the grid, on to the fire; and the trays can be re-used several times if cleaned with care.

Barbecue fan

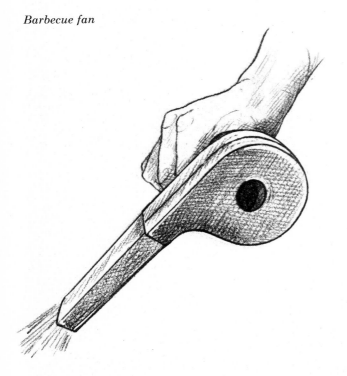

Barbecue fan

Just as it is easier to use an electric hairdryer than sit with your head close to the fire, you may prefer to use a battery-operated fan, which looks very much like a hairdryer, to accelerate lighting the charcoal or briquets with a cunningly applied blast of air. Batteries are not supplied but they last a considerable time as you never need to use the fan for long.

Meat thermometer

If you can't trust your judgement on the degree to which a large joint or bird is done, insert a meat thermometer, which will show how the temperature level has risen in the meat. The thermometer indicates how well various kinds of meat and poultry are cooked according to the temperature it shows. To give an accurate reading, push the thermometer into the thickest part of the flesh. The tip should not rest on a bone, or penetrate the cavity of a bird, such as a turkey.

Wooden-handled skewers

Short skewers are not really recommended. The best type to use is a skewer 16 inches long, notched with fine grooves to hold the food firmly. They can be bought in sets, or separately. Double-pronged skewers hold heavier foods securely for easy turning and there is a small wooden-topped "pusher" you can use to help you remove the food from the skewer without burning your fingers.

Cleaning-up Equipment

One of the tools so often forgotten is a suitable brush for cleaning up after the barbecue is over. Even an elderly scrubbing brush can be used (although it will not be fit for floors afterwards) but a purpose-made tool is infinitely better. The best kind has tough brass bristles, which are really "man enough for the job" with a strong scraper protruding from the bristle end. With this in hand, even the most stubborn burnt-on remnants of food can be removed.

Today it is easier than ever before, because there is an aerosol spray which softens up the grime, if you use it according to the directions on the can. My own experience is that it does not work instantaneously, so be patient and wait a while for it to act.

Salmon Steaks with Basil and Lemon Butter (page 59)

COOKING METHODS

Barbecue cooking is very different from preparing ordinary meals. There are various techniques which need to be mastered, if you are to have sufficient different foods cooked and ready to serve at the same time. The party will hardly be a success if you have warm rolls but no hamburgers to put inside them; or the steaks and chops are nicely cooked but the potatoes are still hard in the center.

Portable Gas Barbecue

Help from your Oven or Microwave

When all is said and done, the cooking area on one barbecue, or even several, is limited. When items take a long time to cook, such as foil parcels containing large potatoes, this precious space is often needed for quick-cooking items such as kebabs or sausages. Even the microwave needs more than a few minutes to cook a number of potatoes, since the power set at high might give you one soft, floury potato in five minutes, but requires as long as twelve to give the same result with four potatoes.

When I have to cook for a dozen or more people, I usually pop a whole trayful of potatoes in my conventional oven an hour or so before they are needed. Use another shelf for cookie sheets spread with fresh pork or beef sausage links, and other good-tempered foods such as chicken drumsticks. Shortly before the barbecue itself is ready for hamburgers, chops and foil parcels of frozen vegetables, that merely need defrosting and reheating, I put these potatoes, four at a time, into the microwave for a mere minute or two. Then I foil-wrap them and simply finish off on the barbecue grid or in the ashes, since they are well softened up and nearly ready to serve.

If the barbecue is not taking place in your garden, but further afield, an old shopping bag or basket lined with crumpled newspaper insulates the parcelled potatoes and keeps them hot for a long time. I use a padded teacosy as a makeshift cover.

Trays of sausage links and drumsticks need not even be switched from the cookie sheet to the grid, providing you've chosen an old cookie sheet that can stand a little rough treatment. Brush the food with yeast extract softened with butter, or with barbecue sauce, so the outside looks invitingly glossy, and let them sizzle away ready to be speared with forks.

Once the oven is clear of potatoes, I often follow up with cored and half-peeled tart apples, but these do need to be foil-wrapped at the start, as they are too soft to wrap when partly cooked.

Any small items including not only sausage links and drumsticks but lamb and pork chops, even chicken quarters, can be given a flying start in the microwave. It is no disadvantage that they will cook without browning on the outside, as they need only be well brushed with a flavorful baste before arranging on the barbecue grid for the authentic crusty finish.

Parcel Cooking

Foods you may have thought rather bland in taste, take on a new excitement when wrapped in foil and cooked over or in the coals. All their delicate flavor, enhanced by seasonings and sauces of your choice, are captured and blended in the parcel. Crimp and seal the edges tightly so that juices cannot possibly ooze out. If the food has to be kept waiting, it keeps warm and moist in the parcel for anything up to an hour, a great advantage if there's a hold-up somewhere in the preparation line. Secure sealing is important because you may decide to turn over the pack half-way through cooking.

Here's a chart to give you some idea of timing:

1-lb. pack of rump steak	20 minutes
Hamburgers	20 minutes
Frankfurters	6 minutes
Chicken portions	$1-1\frac{1}{4}$ hours
Whole chicken (weight $2\frac{1}{2}-3\frac{1}{2}$ lb.)	$1\frac{1}{4}-1\frac{3}{4}$ hours

When parcel-cooking chicken, use poultry shears to snip off any protruding bones that might pierce the pack. Put portions skin-side down on the square of foil, add chopped vegetables, seasoning, 1 tablespoon bouillon or other liquid such as tomato juice, add a small knob of butter or margarine if liked. Fold in and seal over these ingredients. Cook, chicken side down, without turning, so that the skin browns almost as well as if roasted. You can add quick-cooking rice to the vegetables, etc. with a little extra liquid for the rice to absorb, and the resulting parcel is almost a whole meal.

Medium Gas Barbecue

Broiling

Steaks and chops, either lamb or pork, are usually the first choice. These items, which have a fatty edge, are inclined to catch the flames and blacken. Trim off excess fat, snip the edge to prevent curling up, then thread all the trimmings on a skewer. Hold over the heat until they begin to melt, then use the fat to rub on the grid, or the wire grill box if you are using one, so that the steak or chop will not stick to the metal. The thickest piece of meat recommended is $1\frac{1}{2}$ inches. For rare, allow 6 minutes on each side, medium rare 7 minutes per side, medium 8 minutes per side, and well done 12 minutes per side. Try not to pierce the flesh with a fork during cooking, or you may lose some of the juices. Don't sprinkle with salt and pepper before cooking, instead sprinkle seasonings on the browned side when you turn the steak. If you are not too sure about the quality of steak, pound it with a meat tenderizer before you begin cooking it.

Burgers are particularly tasty, but home-made ones do tend to fall apart during cooking. On the barbecue this is a disaster, as broken pieces cannot be retrieved like a solid piece of meat. Whatever your favorite recipe, you may find that adding a little flour holds them together. White or wholewheat flour do the same job. Another aid might be to coat burgers very lightly first in a thin egg-and-water wash, then just a dusting of flour. Well-chilled burgers are less fragile than warm ones.

Broiling over herbs
Delicate herbs will flare up and disappear. However, ones with woody stems, such as rosemary, can be soaked in water and laid over the grid, and the meat or fish placed on top. When the herbs sear they give off a wonderful perfume which impregnates the flesh. Vine trimmings have the same effect.

The Kebab Method

Although all the necessary advice is given in the short introduction to the chapter on this method, or in the recipes themselves, it does need to be borne in mind that you cannot expect success if some of the foods are still raw when others are fully cooked. Here are some helpful tips:
● Whole or firm quartered onions may be plunged into boiling water for just a couple of minutes to blanch and soften them.
● Make sure the items that need the most cooking are centered on the skewer and not pressed too tightly together.
● Mushroom caps can be "sandwiched" together, stem sides inside, putting a tiny knob of butter in the center.

Spit-Roasting

Before you begin, position the drip pan and half-fill it with water; this precaution usually shows you whether the pan sits level. A glass or so of left-over wine could very usefully be added to bring the water to the right height. A drip pan containing nothing but fat is so often responsible for an unexpected flare-up. But it is never good to add water to a pan that has hot fat in it, as it spits.

Setting the food correctly on the spit is very important as the rod should pass through the center of gravity, that is where the weight is evenly distributed on all sides. In order not to put a strain on the motor which rotates your spit, it is essential that it should turn evenly and smoothly rather than in jerks. To check whether you have correctly calculated the balance, rotate the spit by hand before you slip it into its grooves. If it rolls unevenly, try to correct the balance before cooking starts. If there is very limited space between the spit and the coals, check that birds have, if necessary, been trussed into a neat shape. If you are in any doubt that the clamps have not been fully tightened by hand, use a small pair of pliers.

Dealing with small birds
If the birds weigh a minimum of $2-2\frac{1}{4}$ lb, string them nose to tail along the spit. But some game birds, which are ideal for barbecuing, weigh much less. Thread them through the carcass, alternately tail up, head up, and as closely as possible. If the flesh is dry, wrap each one with a slice of fat bacon and tie it on firmly with string, as you would lard a pheasant for oven roasting. By the time the birds

are cooked, the bacon will all but have disappeared, but the flesh of the breasts will be tender.

Sear to Seal

The searing process is much more important when barbecuing than when frying or cooking under a broiler in the kitchen, because once lost, the meat juices have disappeared into the fire. Nothing is left even to make a tasty gravy. Turn until both sides are well sealed, not forgetting the edges, through which juices often leak.

Chicken portions are awkwardly shaped for searing, and may need turning several times to expose all the surfaces to heat. To hasten cooking, begin by placing portions, or split chicken halves, with the inner side, or cavity side, on the grid. This immediately begins to heat the carcass or bony cavity of the bird, which cooks the thicker part of the flesh or skin side, by transmitted heat. Also you have plenty of time to brush the fleshy skin side with barbecue sauce before turning to brown nicely. The advice does not apply so easily to drumsticks, which have to be carefully examined to determine which is the fleshier side. Turkey drumsticks should not be seared but wrapped in bacon slices to keep them moist.

Concertina-Cooking

Long, narrow pieces of food often cook more successfully if threaded, concertina-style, on skewers. For spareribs, have the butcher cut them in half

Turkey Drumsticks Wrapped in Bacon Slices

crossways, an awkward job to do at home, thus forming two long bony strips. Prebake them in your conventional oven at high heat for 15 minutes, or if you want to purge them of fat, parboil instead. String them up like a closed concertina on a spit or really long and strong skewer, as shown in the drawing.

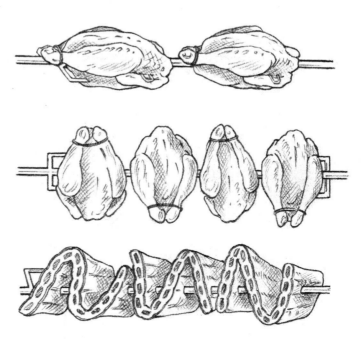

Guide to Barbecue Cooking Times

Fish
Turn carefully half-way through cooking time. Do not overcook.

Whole (8–10 oz.)	10–12 minutes
Whole (8–10 oz.) in foil with vegetables	25–30 minutes
Steaks (1 inch thick)	8–10 minutes
Steaks (1 inch thick) in foil	12–15 minutes
Kebab chunks (about 1-inch cubes)	8–10 minutes

Beef
Turn occasionally during cooking. Best served slightly under-done.

Steaks ($\frac{1}{2}$ inch thick)	4–8 minutes
Steaks (1 inch thick)	5–10 minutes
Hamburgers (1 inch thick)	12–15 minutes
Kebab chunks (about 1-inch cubes)	12–15 minutes

Lamb
Turn occasionally during cooking. Can be served slightly pink if preferred.

Leg bone steaks ($\frac{3}{4}$ inch thick)	20–25 minutes
Boneless double loin chops	20–25 minutes
Loin chops	15–20 minutes
Rib chops	12–15 minutes
Leg or shoulder of lamb (boned and rolled)	Spit roast 20 minutes per 1 lb. or until meat thermometer reads 185–190°F
Spareribs	20 minutes (boil 20 minutes first)
Kebab chunks (about 1-inch cubes)	15–20 minutes

Pork
Turn occasionally during cooking. Always serve well done.

Loin chops	20–25 minutes
Sparerib chops	20–25 minutes
Spareribs	40 minutes
Kebab chunks (about 1-inch cubes)	18–22 minutes

Bacon and ham
Turn frequently during cooking.

Bacon rolls	12–15 minutes
Smoked shoulder butt slices ($\frac{1}{2}$ inch thick)	15–20 minutes
Thick slices of Canadian style bacon ($\frac{1}{2}$ inch thick)	18–25 minutes

Sausage links
Turn frequently but do not prick before cooking.

Large (weight about 2 oz.)	25–30 minutes
Pork links	18–22 minutes

Poultry
Turn and baste frequently during cooking. Always serve well done.

CHICKEN

Breast-and-wing portions	30–40 minutes
Breast-and-wing portions in foil	1 hour
Leg-and-thigh portions	45–55 minutes
Leg-and-thigh portions in foil	1–1$\frac{1}{4}$ hours
Drumsticks	20–25 minutes
Drumsticks in foil	30–35 minutes
Whole chicken (2$\frac{1}{2}$–3$\frac{1}{2}$ lb.)	Covered barbecue or spit-roast 18–20 minutes per 1 lb. or until meat thermometer reads 190°F
Kebab chunks (about 1-inch cubes)	18–22 minutes

TURKEY

Breast fillets (4–5 oz.)	20–25 minutes
Whole turkey (6–8 lb.)	Covered barbecue or spit-roast 20 minutes per 1 lb. or until meat thermometer reads 190°F
Kebab chunks (about 1-inch cubes)	18–22 minutes

DUCK

Breast-and-wing portions	40–45 minutes
Breast-and-wing portions in foil	50–55 minutes plus 5 minutes unwrapped on grid
Leg-and-thigh portions	45–55 minutes
Leg-and-thigh portions in foil	55–65 minutes plus 5 minutes unwrapped on grid
Whole duck (4–5 lb.)	Spit-roast 20 minutes per 1 lb. or until meat thermometer reads 190°F

Since barbecue cooking times can only be approximate, you should always test before serving. The barbecue chef will probably have to accept the portion on which an experiment is carried out as his or her own!

Ways to Barbecue Sausages

To remove the cooked spareribs, use a two-tined carving fork or kitchen fork, pressing down over the skewer to push them off on to a serving dish, inserting the tines over the end nearest the handle. Push steadily forward, with the point of the skewer resting on the dish. Long sausage links can be threaded in the same way, but take care to make the loops even, so that weight is equal on either side.

Barbecuing Fish

Many people who enjoy fish, imagine it must be difficult to cook by any of the traditional barbecue methods, other than wrapping it in a foil parcel. Here are some hints to make it easy, using the direct heat or kebab method:

● Always baste non-oily fish with firm white flesh either with oil or oil flavored with lemon juice, garlic and herbs, to prevent the fish from drying out.

● When cooking very thick whole fish, slash the flesh at its thickest parts to allow the heat to penetrate evenly. Make sure the marinade or baste trickles into the slashes.

● If you possess a wire fish broiler, use it to cook whole fish such as mullet or mackerel so that they can be turned over easily.

● When barbecuing small oily fish, wrap in foil until almost cooked then brown off over the coals. This will ensure that the skin does not become too brown.

● When making kebabs to barbecue, always start and finish the kebab with something firm like an onion, so that the ingredients are held securely in place.

● Make sure the skewer pierces the flesh across the grain, and not between two flakes which might separate and let the fish fall off the skewer.

● Use kebab skewers that are flat, so when you turn them over all the ingredients will not turn around as well.

● Even the more delicate type of fish can be used, such as scallops or rolls of plaice or flounder, but pack tightly on to the skewers so that they do not break up during cooking. Rolls of lemon sole or chunks of whiting can be cooked in the same way.

● The firmer fleshed fish should be loosely threaded on the skewers so that they cook evenly, otherwise the inner part next to the skewer may not be cooked through.

● Small fish can be threaded on long, thin skewers, head to tail, and placed over the barbecue.

● Remember barbecuing is a difficult method in which to control the temperature, so do check frequently that you are not overcooking the fish.

Three Ways to Barbecue Trout

TROUT IN NEWSPAPER

4 (8–10-oz.) trout, cleaned
freshly ground black pepper or lemon pepper
seasoning
1 lemon, sliced

Have ready a large sheet of newspaper for each fish. Wash the trout and dry inside and out with absorbent kitchen paper. Lay one fish on each sheet of newspaper and season inside the cavities with pepper or seasoning. Fill the fish with the lemon slices.

Roll up each sheet of newspaper, enclosing the fish, to make a neat parcel, tucking the ends in firmly. Hold the parcels under running cold water until thoroughly soaked, squeezing out excess gently. Arrange the parcels on the grid. Barbecue for about 25 minutes, turning occasionally, until the paper is dried out.

To serve, snip through the covering and, as you open back the paper, the skin of the trout will come away with it, leaving just the moist flesh. *Serves 4*

Variations

SPICY BROILED TROUT Wash and dry the fish as above. Mix together 1 tablespoon sweet paprika pepper, $1\frac{1}{2}$ teaspoons salt and $\frac{1}{4}$ teaspoon chili powder. Sprinkle about half this mixture inside the cavities of 4 trout, then add 1 teaspoon finely chopped onion to each. Brush the skin of the fish with oil and sprinkle with more of the spice mixture. Arrange the fish on the grid.

Barbecue for about 8 minutes, turning carefully half-way through, brushing the fish with more oil and sprinkling again with spice, until the flesh flakes easily when tested with a fork.

BARBECUE TROUT PROVENÇALE Wash and dry the fish as in the main recipe. Chop fresh herbs such as parsley, thyme, sage and rosemary, to give 5 tablespoons chopped herb, or use $1\frac{1}{2}$ teaspoons dried herbs. Brush the fish inside and out with oil, then sprinkle with the herb mixture and season with salt and pepper to taste. Arrange the fish on the grid. Barbecue for about 8 minutes, turning carefully half-way through cooking, until the flesh flakes easily when tested.

FOODS TO BARBECUE

All the foods you see in the photograph opposite are ideal for the barbecue and, of course, there are many others. But certain basic rules are important when shopping for the provisions, to prevent such disasters as biting into a barbecued piece of meat and finding it hard or rubbery. Let's discuss the items you will probably choose to buy.

Various Foods Suitable for Barbecuing

Fish

Any fish can be cooked, portioned, in parcels. But for placing straight on the barbecue, oily fish such as mullet, mackerel and sardines are ideal. Salmon is more expensive, but well worth it, since the flesh is firm enough to hold together when sliced into steaks; the color is so attractive and the flavor superb. Any white fish that cuts into neat steaks can be used; I suggest cod steaks, snapper, halibut and haddock.

Meat

This has to be tender and quick-cooking. Stewing steak or lamb simply will not do, unless in the form of ground meat for burgers. Fortunately there are excellent cuts in the cheaper range. Besides any kind of steak intended for frying or broiling, you can choose lamb chops, the cutlets which come from the rack, escalopes or leg steaks as they are sometimes called, and that particularly sweet and delicious joint, the shoulder. Boned, it spit-roasts excellently.

Pork is also a perfect choice, because *all* cuts of pork are tender enough to barbecue well. Succulent little pork spareribs, shoulder steaks and chops are universal favorites.

Another word about beef – rump steaks are so splendidly juicy and taste so good, you may decide sometimes to treat yourself to them. Cook in the whole piece and portion up to serve. This gives rare center cuts to those who like the meat pink. Sirloin steaks, cut fairly thin, are less expensive and with care in marinating or basting can turn out just as tender as rump. Beef spareribs are fine. Finely ground good quality beef has a place too, in a kebab mixture (see page 64).

A good general rule on meat is that the firmer the tissue, the more protection it needs. Enclosing in a parcel with tenderizing ingredients (those that will release moisture and thus keep the meat itself moist during cooking) is a great help. Try meat tenderizers if you wish, but they do tend to add flavor rather than make the meat softer. For best results, trim off excess fat and try to have all the items matched in size and thickness.

Variety meats

Liver and lamb kidney barbecue well if threaded on skewers; though beef kidney cannot be recommended, as it will toughen before it's cooked through.

Hamburgers

Today these are almost infinite in their variety. The good old fashioned beef burger, lamb burger, mixed meat burger, are the staples of every barbecue chef. But there are vegetarian burgers and I have included a recipe for these, which I feel even avid meat-eaters will enjoy. When you make up your own burgers, remember that they freeze remarkably well when packed with dividers, so that you can peel off and separate layers as you need them.

Sausage links

Sausages are highly adaptable for grill or kebab cooking. Pork, pork-and-beef, all beef, herbed or even spiced, they all contain sufficient fat for barbecuing and therefore require little attention except frequent turning. Frankfurters really only need reheating, so don't let them dry out and shrivel up.

Bacon and ham

Thinly sliced bacon can be used more safely if rolled up and skewered, otherwise it is inclined to cause a conflagration. However, such items as thick slices of Canadian style bacon and smoked shoulder butt slices sit very neatly on the barbecue, provided you snip fat edges to prevent them curling up. Although tasty in themselves, they take well to all sorts of sauces, especially mustardy ones.

Poultry

Here again, we barbecue enthusiasts are lucky. All cuts of chicken, turkey and duck are easy to cook quickly and keep succulent. Avoid the elderly boiling hen, it does take time and likes to float in a lot of liquid, so isn't conducive to barbecuing. Portions such as a complete thigh and drumstick of chicken, or smaller pieces (drumsticks only, perhaps) cook very quickly and stay moist. With poultry, there's rarely any need to trim off excess fat, but it can be used to grease the grill, as with meat.

Vegetables

Perhaps the best known way is to make these up into foil packs, such as peas packed together with shredded lettuce and chopped onion and seasoned to taste. When space is limited, and it usually is, make the packs portion size, and make good use of frozen vegetables. Then the time taken on the grid is little more than sufficient to defrost and heat the vegetable, and blend all the flavors you have put together. This happens quickly inside a good seal. Some vegetables have their own natural protection and can be placed straight on the grid – possible with eggplants and zucchini. But often they are nicer halved, possibly par-boiled, and stuffed with the center flesh and other ingredients; then par-celled and finished off over moderate heat for 20 minutes or so. All these methods can be started off in a conventional oven or microwave, then trans-ported to the barbecue site. Potatoes, coming naturally ready to cook in their own jackets, do seem destined for cooking on the grid. But thick slices can be barbecued if liberally coated with oil (see page 104).

Fruit

If firm, halves or thick slices of fruit can be skewered, brushed with melted light corn syrup or a spicy glaze based on brown sugar, and quickly barbecued. Fruit tends to fall off the skewer if this is not done speedily, although a sugary glaze does help to keep the fruit pieces whole. Entire fruit such as apples can be cooked in foil parcels, or used in slices to dip in a fondue (see page 110). My advised best buys are: apples, bananas, tenderized dried apricots, canned pineapple rings. For dipping, choose from whole strawberries, pieces of Kiwi fruit, pieces of fresh pineapple or nectarine and, of course, the ever useful banana. Fruit which tend to discolor should be lightly tossed in lemon juice to keep the flesh from becoming brown.

INTRODUCTION TO RECIPES

Barbecues are such fun events, they develop into parties, whether planned just for the family or a group of friends. People naturally gather round, anxious to help and join in the work. So the barbecue cook isn't often condemned to lonely isolation in the kitchen, preparing a big meal. There might even be a surplus of volunteers! Find jobs for them all. Once the fire is well alight and glowing, for example let someone open up packs of rolls and buns to warm before being filled with succulent burgers. Put another helper in charge of the salads, or setting out the dressings and sauces. A whole team might be happily occupied threading kebab skewers with ingredients in the right order, or creating individual masterpieces.

Glance through these colorful pages and discover the wide selection of fascinating new recipes they contain, to expand your repertoire and gain greater expertise in the art of barbecue cooking.

Most of the fish, meat and poultry recipes already include special marinades, bastes or sauces. To substitute a different flavor you particularly enjoy, turn to our section on sauces and try something different. Be adventurous with salads too, if you have time to shop ahead for exciting ingredients, then give a thought to the end of the meal, to introduce some sweet surprises.

BROILING

This is the most commonly used method of
barbecue cooking and in many ways it is the easiest.
Certainly there is no preliminary work
needed, such as wrapping in foil or threading food
on skewers. Pieces that will lie fairly flat
on the grid and are no thicker than 2 inches
are ideal for broiling. Thicker items may need a
"tent" of foil over the exposed surface
to ensure cooking through to the center.
This way of barbecuing is not only simple
and quick, but imparts a delicious
crusty exterior to all kinds of meat, poultry
and fish, and especially to everyone's
favorite, the ubiquitous hamburger.

Pork Rib Chops with Tomato Pepper Sauce (page 61)

RELISHBURGERS

2 cups white bread crumbs
2¼ lb. ground beef
4 tablespoons bottled barbecue relish
1 large onion, finely chopped
1 egg
rolled oats for coating

For the garnish:

parsley sprigs

Add the bread crumbs to the meat, relish, onion and egg in a bowl and mix thoroughly. Divide into 12 equal portions and shape each into a burger about 1 inch thick. Coat with oats, patting them on well.

Line a cookie sheet with foil, put the relish-burgers on top, cover with more foil and crimp all round to make an airtight parcel. Chill thoroughly before cooking.

Unwrap and arrange the chilled burgers on the oiled grid. Barbecue for about 15 minutes, turning carefully half-way through cooking. Garnish with parsley and serve in buns accompanied by a cucumber salad and more relish. *Serves 12*
Note: These burgers can be foil-wrapped and frozen very successfully. Defrost before cooking.

SMOKED SLICES WITH CHERRY BARBECUE SAUCE

4 (4-oz.) smoked shoulder slices
salt and freshly ground black pepper
oil
1 clove of garlic
1 medium-sized onion, finely chopped
1 tablespoon cornstarch
1 (15-oz.) can pitted red cherries
5 tablespoons bottled barbecue sauce

Season the slices with salt and pepper.

Put 3 tablespoons oil in a pan and use to fry the garlic and onion until softened. Moisten the cornstarch with a little of the cherry syrup and add the remainder to the pan with the cherries and barbecue sauce. Stir until boiling, add the cornstarch mixture and continue stirring until thickened. Keep hot in the covered pan on the side of the barbecue until the slices are cooked.

Place the shoulder slices on the greased grid.

Barbecue for about 10 minutes, turning half-way through cooking. Serve with the cherry barbecue sauce. *Serves 4*

Variation
TURKEY FILLETS WITH CHERRY BARBECUE SAUCE Substitute 4 (4-oz.) turkey breast fillets for the shoulder slices. After seasoning, enclose each fillet in a sheet of oiled foil to make an airtight parcel. Place on the grid and barbecue for about 30 minutes, turning the parcels occasionally. Serve with the sauce as in the main recipe.

HERBY CHICKEN FINGERS

Illustrated on page 69

2 boneless chicken breasts, skinned
¾ cup finely crushed cornflakes
½ teaspoon dried thyme
finely grated rind of ½ lemon
1 egg, beaten

For serving:

lemon wedges
RED CURRANT SWEET AND SOUR SAUCE (see page 99)

Cut the chicken breasts into ½-inch wide strips with a sharp knife. Put the cornflakes into a bowl and add the thyme and lemon rind. Place the egg in a shallow dish.

Dip the chicken strips in the egg and then coat all over with the cornflake mixture, pressing it on firmly. Place the coated chicken fingers on a cookie sheet lined with foil and chill for at least 2 hours.

Arrange the chicken on the greased grid. Barbecue for about 10 minutes, turning frequently, until deep golden brown. Serve with lemon wedges and RED CURRANT SWEET AND SOUR SAUCE as a dip. *Serves 4*

Variation
CRUNCHY PORK STRIPS Substitute 1 large pork tenderloin for the chicken breasts and cut into strips as above. Make up the cornflake coating, using orange rind in place of the lemon rind and ¼ teaspoon dried sage instead of the thyme. Coat the strips and barbecue as above.

Left: Relishburgers. Right: Smoked Slices with Cherry Barbecue Sauce

BLUE CHEESE CHICKEN

6 chicken breasts
⅔ cup Italian dressing
salt and freshly ground black pepper
⅓ cup butter
1 cup finely crumbled blue cheese
1 tablespoon snipped chives
1 clove of garlic, finely chopped
3 tablespoons brandy

For the garnish:

sprigs of mint or watercress
lime or lemon wedges

Place the chicken breasts in a shallow dish, spoon the dressing over them and sprinkle lightly with salt and pepper. Cover and chill for 4 hours, turning the chicken pieces once during this time.

Meanwhile, soften the butter and mix with the cheese, chives, garlic and brandy and season with salt and pepper to taste. Place on a sheet of foil or plastic wrap and form into a roll about 1 inch in diameter. Chill until firm.

Drain the chicken breasts and place on the greased grid, skin side upwards. Barbecue for about 10 minutes. Take half the cheese butter and cut into 12 pieces. Place one piece on each chicken breast and cook for a further 5 minutes. Turn the breasts, put a piece of butter on each and continue barbecuing for a further 15 minutes, or until juices run clear when tested.

Cut the remaining cheese butter into 6 pieces. Arrange the cooked chicken breasts on a serving dish, top each with a piece of cheese butter and allow this to melt. Garnish with herbs and lime or lemon wedges. *Serves 6*

Blue Cheese Chicken

CURRIED VEGETABLE AND NUT BURGERS

1 cup roast salted peanuts, chopped
2 cups fresh wholewheat bread crumbs
$\frac{1}{3}$ cup chopped sweet green pepper
1 medium-sized onion, chopped
1 cup mushrooms, sliced
1 egg, beaten
$\frac{1}{2}$ teaspoon dried basil
$\frac{1}{2}$ teaspoon dried parsley
1 tablespoon bottled curry sauce

For the coating:

$\frac{1}{2}$ cup all-purpose flour

Curried Vegetable and Nut Burgers, Brown Rice Salad (page 96)

Place the peanuts, bread crumbs, pepper, onion and mushrooms together in a blender or food processor and switch on briefly. The ingredients should be finely chopped but not smooth. Transfer to a bowl and add half the egg, the herbs and curry sauce. Mix well.

Divide the mixture into 8 equal portions and shape each into a round flat cake. Coat the burgers in the remaining egg then cover all over in flour.

Arrange the burgers on the greased grid. Barbecue for 10 minutes, turning them carefully halfway through. Serve with BROWN RICE SALAD (see page 96) and crusty rolls. *Serves 8*

ONION SMOTHERED BACON SLICES

6 ($\frac{1}{2}$-inch) slices Canadian style bacon
1$\frac{1}{4}$ cups dark beer
freshly ground black pepper
1 bay leaf
3 medium-sized onions, sliced
3 tablespoons molasses
1 tablespoon lemon juice
3 tablespoons oil

Put the slices in a shallow dish and pour over the beer. Sprinkle with pepper, add the bay leaf and a third of the onion slices. Chill for at least 8 hours.

Drain the marinade into a pan and boil until reduced by half. Stir in the molasses and lemon juice.

Heat the oil and use to fry the remaining onion slices until beginning to soften. Set aside.

Arrange the bacon slices on the greased grid. Barbecue for 10 minutes, brushing frequently with the beer baste. Turn the slices, brush again, top with fried onion rings and spoon over more of the baste. Cook for a further 10 minutes, or until the slices are tender and glazed. Serve with a tomato salad and baked potatoes or BARBECUED POTATO SLICES (see page 104). *Serves 6*

Onion Smothered Bacon Slices

HARVEST BURGERS

1 eating apple, cored
1 lb. extra lean ground beef
1 medium-sized onion, finely chopped
1$\frac{1}{2}$ cups Nutrigrain (wholewheat and raisins), finely crushed
1 teaspoon Worcestershire sauce
2 teaspoons ground coriander
1 egg, beaten
salt and freshly ground black pepper

Grate the apple into a bowl and add the meat, onion, cereal, Worcestershire sauce and coriander. Combine the ingredients, add the egg and season with salt and pepper to taste. Mix well.

Divide the mixture into 4 equal portions. Shape each into a 3$\frac{1}{2}$-inch square, $\frac{1}{2}$ inch thick, using 2 wet round-bladed knives to get a good angular shape. Cut each square in half diagonally to form 2 triangles. Place on a cookie sheet lined with foil and chill for at least 1 hour.

Arrange the burgers on the greased grid. Barbecue for 15 minutes, turning them about 4 times during cooking, until done to taste. Serve in triangular BRAN ROLLS (see page 108). *Serves 8*

Harvest Burgers, Bran Rolls (page 108)

ROQUEFORT-TOPPED HAM SLICES

$\frac{1}{3}$ cup butter, softened
1 cup crumbled Roquefort cheese
salt and freshly ground black pepper
6 scallions, trimmed
pared rind and juice of 2 oranges
4 (5-oz.) thick smoked ham slices
little oil

For the garnish:

4 orange slices
sprigs of parsley

First make the blue cheese butter. Beat together the butter and cheese and season with salt and pepper to taste. Place on a sheet of foil and form into a roll. Chill until firm.

Slice the onions and cut the orange rind into fine shreds. Stir both into the orange juice and set aside.

Snip the fat of the slices at regular intervals to keep them flat during cooking. Brush on both sides with oil. Place in a large pan or on an old cookie sheet. Cook on the barbecue for 10 minutes. Turn the slices, spoon over the orange juice and onion mixture and continue cooking for a further 10 minutes, or until the ham is tender.

Cut the cheese butter into 4 slices. Serve each ham slice garnished with a slice of orange, a slice of cheese butter and a sprig of parsley. *Serves 4*

FARM BURGERS

1 tablespoon oil
3 scallions, finely chopped
1 lb. ground pork and lamb combined
1 cup fresh wholewheat bread crumbs
1 teaspoon chopped fresh parsley
1 teaspoon dried mixed herbs
1 small egg, beaten
1 tablespoon white wine or water
$\frac{1}{2}$ teaspoon Lo Salt (low sodium salt)
$\frac{1}{4}$ teaspoon pepper

Heat the oil and use to fry the scallions gently until soft. Drain well and mix the onion with the meat, bread crumbs and herbs. Combine the egg, liquid, low sodium salt and pepper, add to the meat mixture and work the ingredients together. Divide

into 8 equal portions and shape into thin burgers.

Arrange the burgers on the greased grid. Barbecue for 4–5 minutes on each side, or until done to taste. Serve with a fresh tomato sauce, seasoned with low sodium salt, and a green salad. *Serves 4*
Note: This recipe is particularly suitable for people who wish to limit their salt intake.

LAMB AND PEANUT BURGERS

Illustrated on page 2

1 lb. ground raw lamb
1 medium-sized onion, chopped
$\frac{1}{3}$ cup chopped dry roasted peanuts
$\frac{1}{2}$ teaspoon dried mixed herbs
salt and freshly ground black pepper
little oil

For serving:

6 teaspoons peanut butter, smooth or crunchy
6 hamburger buns
3 tomatoes, sliced

Put the lamb, onion, chopped peanuts and herbs into a bowl and season with salt and pepper to taste. Mix well. Divide the mixture into 6 equal portions and shape each into a burger.

Brush the burgers with oil and arrange on the greased grid. Barbecue for about 15 minutes, turning half-way through the cooking time.

Meanwhile, spread the peanut butter on the buns and top with tomato slices. Serve a burger in each bun and hand SOUTH SEA and FRESH HERB SAUCES separately. *Serves 6*

Accompaniments
SOUTH SEA SAUCE Mix together 1 tablespoon mild mustard, 3 tablespoons chopped preserved ginger and 3 tablespoons lemon juice. Mash 1 banana and drain 1 ($13\frac{1}{2}$-oz.) can crushed pineapple. Stir these into the mustard mixture and transfer to a small bowl. Serve with the burgers.
FRESH HERB SAUCE Deseed $\frac{1}{2}$ small sweet green pepper and chop the flesh very finely. Mix with 1 tablespoon chopped tarragon, 2 teaspoons snipped chives, 3 tablespoons tomato paste and $\frac{2}{3}$ cup mayonnaise. Serve with the burgers.

Roquefort-Topped Ham Slices

PORK CHOPS PROVENÇALE

4 pork loin chops

For the sauce:

1 (8-oz.) can tomatoes
1 small onion, finely chopped
3 tablespoons white wine
1 tablespoon tomato paste
1 teaspoon sweet paprika pepper
1 teaspoon dried mixed herbs
1 teaspoon oil

First make the sauce. Drain the tomatoes, reserving the liquid. Chop the tomatoes and combine with the remaining sauce ingredients in a bowl. Stir in about 3 tablespoons of the reserved tomato liquid.

Brush the chops on both sides with the sauce and arrange on the greased grid. Barbecue for about 25 minutes, turning occasionally and brushing with more of the sauce until cooked through. Heat the remaining sauce and serve with the barbecued chops and a salad. *Serves 6*

LAMB CHOPS WITH RICH APPLE SAUCE

6 loin of lamb chops
oil

For the sauce:

2 large tart apples
1 medium-sized onion, chopped
$\frac{2}{3}$ cup tomato catsup
3 tablespoons light brown sugar
$\frac{1}{4}$ cup butter or margarine
salt and freshly ground black pepper

First make the barbecue sauce. Peel, core and chop the apples. Place in a pan with the onion, catsup, sugar and butter, and stir until boiling. Simmer for 3 minutes, then season with salt and pepper.

Brush the chops with oil and arrange on the greased grid. Barbecue for 10 minutes, turning once. Brush the chops with the sauce and barbecue for about a further 5 minutes on each side, or until the coating looks glazed and the chops are cooked. Hand the remaining sauce separately. *Serves 6*

Pork Chops Provençale

52

CHICKEN WITH SWEET AND SOUR TOMATO SAUCE

8 chicken drumsticks or thighs
1 tablespoon clear honey
1 tablespoon sweet fruit chutney, chopped
if necessary
3 tablespoons vinegar
3 tablespoons lemon juice
pinch of garlic granules
1 teaspoon barbecue spice
1 (10½-oz.) can condensed tomato soup

Put the chicken pieces into a shallow dish. Mix together the honey, chutney, vinegar, lemon juice, garlic granules and barbecue spice. Spoon the mixture over the chicken, turning the pieces until coated. Cover and leave to stand for at least 2 hours.

Drain the marinade into a small pan and stir in the soup. Bring to boiling point, stirring.

Arrange the chicken pieces on the greased grid. Barbecue drumsticks for about 25 minutes and thighs for about 30 minutes, turning them occasionally and brushing with the sauce during cooking. Reheat the remaining sauce in the pan on the barbecue and use to accompany the cooked chicken. Serve a warm pasta salad with this succulent dish. *Serves 4*

CRANBERRY ORANGE SPARERIBS

4 pork spareribs
1 (6½-oz.) jar cranberry orange sauce
4 tablespoons soy sauce
1 teaspoon chili sauce
1 clove of garlic, finely chopped
salt and freshly ground black pepper

For the garnish:

orange slices
sprigs of watercress

Put the spareribs in a shallow dish. Mash the cranberry sauce and combine with the soy sauce, chili sauce and garlic. Season lightly with salt and pepper to taste and spoon over the pork. Cover and chill for 4 hours, turning the chops occasionally.

Drain the marinade mixture into a pan and bring to boiling point, stirring frequently. Simmer for 3

minutes. Keep warm on the side of the barbecue while cooking the meat.

Arrange the spareribs on the greased grid. Barbecue for about 12 minutes each side, or until cooked through.

Transfer the sauce to a dish and place on a serving platter. Surround with the spareribs, spoon a little sauce over each and serve garnished with orange slices and watercress sprigs. *Serves 4*

RICE AND BEEF BURGERS

1 lb. ground beef
½ teaspoon dried mixed herbs
1 small onion, finely chopped
1 cup cooked long grain rice
1 egg, beaten
salt and freshly ground black pepper
little cornstarch for coating
oil

Mix together the meat, herbs, onion, rice and egg and season with salt and pepper to taste. Cover the mixture and leave to stand for 30 minutes.

Divide into 6 equal portions and form each into a burger, using a mold if possible and pressing the ingredients well together. Dust lightly with cornstarch and brush with oil before cooking.

Arrange the burgers on the well greased grid. Barbecue for about 15 minutes, turning carefully half-way through cooking. Serve with a green salad and relish. *Serves 6*

Variations
RICE AND PORK BURGERS Substitute ground pork for the beef and use dried sage in place of the mixed herbs. Serve with apple sauce and CARROT AND RAISIN SALAD (see page 99).
RICE AND LAMB BURGERS Substitute ground lamb for the beef and use ½ teaspoon ground allspice in place of the mixed herbs. Serve with sweet mint jelly and FENNEL AND ORANGE SALAD (see page 95).
RICE AND SAUSAGE BURGERS Substitute bulk pork sausage for the beef and use 2 tablespoons chopped fresh parsley in place of the dried mixed herbs. Serve with beans in barbecue sauce.
Barbecue cooking times for all these burgers should be about the same.

Mustardy Mackerel

MUSTARDY MACKEREL

1 (15-oz.) can borlotti beans, drained
4 tablespoons bottled mild mustard sauce
4 scallions, trimmed and chopped
5 tablespoons finely chopped mixed herbs
sea salt and freshly ground black pepper
4 medium-sized mackerel, cleaned
4 stalks of celery, thinly sliced
5 tablespoons vinaigrette dressing

For the garnish:

2 tomatoes, halved

Rinse the beans with cold water if necessary and drain again. Take 5 tablespoons of the beans and mix with half the sauce, the onion and herbs. Season with salt and pepper to taste and use to stuff the mackerel.

Brush the stuffed fish with half the remaining sauce and arrange in a foil grill tray. Barbecue for about 10 minutes then turn the fish carefully. Brush with the remaining sauce and continue cooking for a further 10 minutes, or until the flesh flakes easily when tested with a fork. Garnish with the tomato halves.

Combine the remaining beans with the celery and vinaigrette and serve with the fish. *Serves 4*

Pork Steaks with Pineapple Crowns

PORK STEAKS WITH PINEAPPLE CROWNS

1 tablespoon light brown sugar
1 (15-oz.) can pineapple slices in syrup
(8 slices are required)
10 tablespoons bottled barbecue relish
1 canned red pimento, chopped
8 pork steaks

Dissolve the sugar in the pineapple syrup in a pan and boil until reduced by half. Put half the relish in a small heatproof bowl or pan and stir in the reduced syrup and pimento. Keep warm on the barbecue.

Arrange the steaks on the greased grid and brush the tops with the relish mixture. Barbecue over medium heat for 12 minutes, turn and brush again with the relish mixture. Top each steak with a pineapple slice, brush this also with the mixture and barbecue for a further 12 minutes, or until the steaks are cooked through.

Spoon the remaining relish into the center of the pineapple slices. Serve with a leafy green salad, the rest of the sauce and baked potatoes. *Serves 8*

Variation

HAM WITH PEACH CUPS Substitute 8 (4-oz.) smoked ham steaks for the pork steaks and use a can of peach halves instead of the pineapple slices. Cut a sliver from the rounded side of each peach half so that it will stand firmly on a ham steak. Omit the sugar and boil the syrup until reduced by just one third before adding to the relish.

BUTTERFLIED LEG OF LAMB

Illustrated on page 6

1 (4½-lb.) leg of lamb, boned

For the marinade:

⅔ cup white wine
5 tablespoons oil
finely grated rind and juice of 1 lemon
2 cloves of garlic, finely chopped
¼ cup light soft brown sugar
salt and freshly ground black pepper

Open the boned leg of lamb out flat to form a butterfly shape and place in a dish.

Mix together the wine, oil, lemon rind and juice, the garlic and sugar. Season with salt and pepper to taste and pour over the lamb. Cover and leave to stand for at least 4 hours, turning the meat once.

Remove the leg of lamb from the marinade and position on the grid. Barbecue for about 1 hour, turning frequently and brushing with more of the marinade during cooking, until ready. *Serves 6*

STEAKS WITH HOT SAUCE AND BARBECUE FRIED RICE

4 rumps steaks, about 1 inch thick
little olive oil
salt and freshly ground black pepper

For the sauce:

⅔ cup tomato catsup
5 tablespoons olive oil
3 tablespoons Worcestershire sauce
few drops of hot pepper sauce
1 tablespoon lemon juice

For the fried rice:

4 bacon slices
5 tablespoons peanut or corn oil
1 medium-sized onion, thinly sliced
generous 1 cup long grain rice, cooked
4 eggs, beaten
4 scallions, trimmed and chopped

First make the sauce. Place the catsup, oil, Worcestershire sauce, hot pepper sauce and lemon juice in a pan and heat, stirring, until warm and blended. Transfer to a serving bowl.

Brush the steaks with oil and season with salt and pepper to taste. Arrange on the greased grid. Barbecue for about 1 minute on each side to seal. Brush again with oil and continue cooking for a further 4–5 minutes on each side, until done to taste.

Meanwhile, prepare the fried rice. Cut the bacon into strips. Heat the oil in a skillet on the barbecue and use to fry the onion slices and bacon strips until the bacon is golden. Add the rice and heat through, stirring. When piping hot, pour in the egg and mix well until set. Season generously with salt and pepper to taste and sprinkle on the chopped scallions. Serve hot from the pan. *Serves 4*

MOLASSES BASTED CHICKEN DRUMSTICKS

6 chicken drumsticks

For the sauce:

5 tablespoons vinegar
1 tablespoon molasses sugar
1 tablespoon Worcestershire sauce
1 tablespoon tomato paste
1 teaspoon sweet paprika pepper
salt and freshly ground black pepper

First make the sauce. Put the vinegar, sugar, Worcestershire sauce, tomato paste and paprika in a small pan and bring to simmering point, stirring all the time. Allow to simmer very gently for 10 minutes. Season with salt and pepper to taste.

Make slits in the drumsticks with a sharp knife and brush them all over with the sauce. Place the drumsticks on the greased grid. Barbecue for about 30 minutes, turning occasionally and brushing with more of the sauce until cooked through when tested. *Serves 6*

Variation

SPICY SAUSAGES Substitute 6 large pork or beef sausage links for the chicken drumsticks and use ground mace instead of the paprika. Barbecuing time will be about the same as for the drumsticks but sausages need turning more frequently.

HONEYED DUCK PORTIONS

4 duck breast portions
5 tablespoons clear honey
3 tablespoons oil
3 tablespoons orange juice
1 clove of garlic, crushed
1 tablespoon finely chopped fresh root ginger
$\frac{1}{4}$ teaspoon freshly ground black pepper
salt

For the garnish:

tomato "waterlilies"
sprigs of parsley

Remove the skin from the duck portions and cut 3–4 slashes in the flesh of each. Place in a shallow dish. Combine the honey, oil, orange juice, garlic, ginger and pepper, and spoon over the duck

portions. Cover and chill for at least 8 hours, turning the portions occasionally.

Arrange the duck pieces on the greased grid. Barbecue for about 40 minutes, basting occasionally with the marinade, until the juices run clear when tested. Arrange on a platter, sprinkle lightly with salt, garnish and serve. *Serves 4*

Variations

HONEYED CHICKEN BREASTS Substitute 4 chicken breasts for the duck portions and use pineapple juice in place of the orange juice. Barbecue for about 15 minutes each side.
HONEYED TURKEY FILLETS Substitute 4 (5-oz.) turkey fillets for the duck portions and use apple juice in place of the orange juice. Barbecue for about 10 minutes each side.

HOT STEAKETTES

1 lb. ground beef
1 small onion, finely chopped
1 teaspoon dry mustard powder
2 teaspoons soy sauce
$\frac{1}{4}$ teaspoon barbecue spice
oil

For serving:

4 toasted buns
shredded lettuce
sliced radishes

Mix together the beef, onion, mustard, soy sauce and barbecue spice and divide into 4 equal portions. Shape each into a flat oval shape, pressing the ingredients together. Transfer to a cookie sheet lined with foil, cover and chill well.

Brush the steakettes with oil and arrange on the greased grid. Barbecue for about 14 minutes, turning half-way through cooking time, until done to taste. Fill the toasted buns with lettuce and radish slices and slip in the steakettes. *Serves 4 Note: If good quality beef is used to make these steakettes, they can be served rare if liked. Reduce barbecuing time to 10–12 minutes.*

SPICY FRANKFURTERS Score frankfurter sausages diagonally with a sharp knife and sprinkle barbecue spice into the cuts. Brush the sausages lightly with oil and arrange on the greased grid. Barbecue for about 8 minutes, turning occasionally, until piping hot.

MIXED BROIL WITH MARMALADE GLAZE

selection of meat cuts such as:
loin of pork chops, boneless pork barbecue
chops, loin of lamb chops, $\frac{1}{2}$-inch thick Canadian
bacon or smoked ham slices

For the glaze:

$\frac{1}{2}$ cup marmalade, sieved if preferred
1 tablespoon lemon juice
3 tablespoons oil
1 teaspoon ground cinnamon
4 tablespoons dry sherry

First make the glaze. Put the marmalade, lemon juice, oil and cinnamon in a small pan and heat, stirring, until smooth. Remove from the heat and blend in the sherry.

Trim the cuts of meat if necessary and slash any fat which is around the outside. This will help to keep the meat flat during cooking. Brush well with glaze and arrange on the greased grid. Barbecue for approximate times given, brushing occasionally with the glaze, until cooked to taste. *Makes enough glaze for about 12 cuts of meat*

GUIDE TO BARBECUE COOKING TIMES
Pork loin chops   25–30 minutes
Boneless pork barbecue chops   15–20 minutes
Loin of lamb chops   20–25 minutes
Lamb cutlets   15–20 minutes
Bacon or ham slices   15–20 minutes

BEACH BARBECUED MULLET OR SNAPPER

Illustrated on page 25

3 (8–10-oz.) red or grey mullet or snapper,
cleaned
salt and freshly ground black pepper
1 small onion, sliced
3 sprigs of thyme
3 tablespoons lemon juice
3 tablespoons butter, melted

Wash the fish and dry inside and out with absorbent kitchen paper. Sprinkle the cavities with salt and pepper to taste, add a few onion slices and a sprig of thyme to each.

Heat together the lemon juice and butter and season with salt and pepper to taste. Brush the fish all over with lemon butter and enclose in a wire fish broiler.

Place the fish on the grid. Barbecue for about 8 minutes on each side, turning and brushing with more lemon butter during cooking, until the flesh flakes easily when tested with a fork. Serve with lemon wedges and crusty bread. *Serves 3*

SALMON STEAKS WITH BASIL AND LEMON BUTTER

Illustrated on page 27

1 lemon
1 tablespoon chopped basil or 1 teaspoon
dried basil
$\frac{1}{4}$ cup butter, softened
salt and freshly ground black pepper
4 (6-oz.) salmon steaks
little oil

Pare a few fine strips of lemon rind and cut into shreds. Finely grate the remaining lemon rind and squeeze the juice. Beat the basil, lemon juice and grated rind into the butter and season with salt and pepper to taste. Place on a sheet of foil and gather the herb butter into a ball. Chill well.

Brush the salmon steaks with oil and place on the greased grid. Barbecue for 5 minutes, turn the steaks carefully and cook for a further 4 minutes. Place a quarter of the herb butter on each steak, top with shreds of lemon rind and serve. *Serves 4*

Variations

SALMON WITH ORANGE AND TARRAGON BUTTER Substitute 1 orange for the lemon and use tarragon instead of the basil. Pour half the orange juice over the salmon steaks in a dish and leave to stand for 1 hour before cooking. Make the herb butter with the remaining orange juice.

SALMON, MUSHROOM AND MARJORAM PARCELS Substitute marjoram for the basil to make the herb butter. Place each salmon steak on a sheet of foil. Slice $1\frac{1}{2}$ cups button mushrooms, place on the steaks, sprinkle with salt, pepper and ground nutmeg, then dot with the herb butter. Fold up the foil and crimp the edges to make airtight parcels. Place on the grid and barbecue for about 15 minutes. Sprinkle with the lemon rind shreds.

SPARERIBS WITH SWEET AND SOUR TOMATO SAUCE

$3\frac{1}{4}$ lb. pork spareribs
2 teaspoons ground mixed spice
1 teaspoon ground ginger
1 teaspoon salt
$\frac{1}{4}$ teaspoon pepper
1 tablespoon sugar
$\frac{1}{4}$ teaspoon garlic salt
1 teaspoon dry mustard powder

For the sauce:

1 ($10\frac{1}{2}$-oz.) can condensed cream of tomato soup
3 tablespoons vinegar
1 tablespoon Worcestershire sauce
1 tablespoon soy sauce
3 tablespoons mango chutney, chopped
1 tablespoon dried rosemary

For this recipe, it is easier if the ribs are left in sections until cooking is complete.

Place the spareribs in a shallow container. Combine the mixed spices, ginger, salt, pepper, sugar, garlic salt and mustard powder and sprinkle evenly over the ribs. Rub into the meat and leave to stand for at least 2 hours.

Mix together all the sauce ingredients in a small pan. Place on the barbecue, stirring, until warm.

Arrange the rib sections on the greased grid. Barbecue for about 40 minutes, brushing generously with the sauce and turning now and then. The ribs are cooked when the meat separates easily from the bones. Cut between the ribs before serving with the remaining sauce. *Serves 6–8*

SWEET AND SOUR SPARERIBS

$2\frac{1}{4}$ lb. pork spareribs

For the sauce:

$\frac{2}{3}$ cup cider vinegar
2 teaspoons Dijon mustard
4 tablespoons light brown sugar
4 tablespoons Worcestershire sauce
6 tablespoons tomato paste
4 tablespoons lemon juice
1 small onion, finely chopped
salt and freshly ground black pepper

Make slits in the meat on the ribs with a sharp pointed knife, then lay them in a large shallow dish. Put all the ingredients for the sauce, except the seasoning, in a pan and stir until boiling. Simmer for 10 minutes, then season with salt and pepper to taste. Pour the sauce over the ribs and leave to stand until cool.

Lift out the spareribs and arrange on the greased grid. Barbecue for about 40 minutes, turning and basting frequently with more sauce, until the meat will easily pull away from the bones and the surface is well glazed. *Serves 4–5*

DEVIL'S FIERY DRUMSTICKS

8 chicken drumsticks
2 teaspoons salt
2 teaspoons sugar
1 teaspoon pepper
1 teaspoon ground ginger
1 teaspoon dry mustard powder
$\frac{1}{2}$ teaspoon curry powder
$\frac{1}{4}$ cup butter, melted

For the sauce:

3 tablespoons tomato catsup
1 tablespoon mushroom ketchup
1 tablespoon Worcestershire sauce
1 tablespoon soy sauce
1 tablespoon plum jam
4 drops hot pepper sauce

Slash the flesh of the chicken drumsticks with a sharp knife and place in a shallow dish. Mix together the salt, sugar, pepper, ginger, mustard and curry powder and sprinkle over the drumsticks, turning them until evenly coated. Cover and leave to stand for at least 1 hour.

Brush the chicken with butter. Combine any remaining butter with all the sauce ingredients. Heat, stirring, until blended.

Arrange the buttered drumsticks on the greased grid. Barbecue for about 30 minutes, turning frequently and brushing occasionally with the sauce if liked, until cooked through when tested.

Transfer to a platter, spoon a little sauce over each chicken drumstick and serve the remainder separately. Plenty of fluffy boiled rice is the best accompaniment to these spicy drumsticks and sauce. *Serves 4*

PORK RIB CHOPS WITH TOMATO PEPPER SAUCE

Illustrated on page 42

6 pork rib chops

For the marinade:

$\frac{1}{2}$ cup oil
4 tablespoons white wine vinegar
1 tablespoon chopped fresh parsley
2 cloves of garlic, finely chopped

For the sauce:

1 sweet green pepper, deseeded
1 tablespoon oil
1 medium-sized onion, finely chopped
1 tablespoon tomato paste
1 (14-oz.) can tomatoes
1 teaspoon sugar
few drops of Worcestershire sauce
salt and freshly ground black pepper
2 teaspoons cornstarch
1 tablespoon water

For serving:

shredded lettuce

Lay the chops in a shallow dish. Mix together the ingredients for the marinade, spoon over the pork then cover and leave to stand for at least 4 hours.

Meanwhile, make the sauce. Cut the pepper into thin strips. Heat the oil in a pan and use to fry the onion and pepper until soft. Add the tomato paste, tomatoes and liquid from the can, the sugar, Worcestershire sauce and season with a little salt and pepper. Stir until boiling and simmer for 15 minutes. Blend the cornstarch with the water, stir into the sauce until thickened then adjust the seasoning if necessary. Keep warm on the side of the barbecue while cooking the pork.

Drain the chops and arrange on the greased grid. Barbecue for 12 minutes on each side, brushing with more of the marinade during cooking.

Arrange a bed of lettuce on a serving dish, top with the cooked chops and spoon a little sauce over each. Hand the remaining sauce separately. *Serves 6*

EASY BARBECUED SPARERIBS

1 ($1\frac{1}{2}$-oz.) pack barbecue sauce mix
$1\frac{1}{4}$ cups orange or pineapple juice
5 tablespoons clear honey
1 medium-sized onion, finely chopped
2 cloves of garlic, finely chopped
4 lb. pork spareribs

Place the sauce mix, fruit juice, honey, onion and garlic in a pan and stir until boiling. Leave to cool.

Arrange the spareribs in a shallow layer in 2 large dishes and spoon the sauce evenly over them. Cover and leave in a cool place for 24 hours, turning the ribs occasionally during this time.

Lift out the ribs and place on the greased grid. Barbecue over medium heat for about 40 minutes, turning and brushing frequently with more of the sauce. The ribs are ready when the meat will easily pull away from the bones. Heat any remaining sauce to serve with the ribs, which are delicious accompanied by a crisp coleslaw. *Serves 6–8*
Note: If preferred, transfer the marinated ribs to a large greased roasting pan and cook in a moderate oven (350°F) for 1 hour, then barbecue for about 12–15 minutes, until glazed. Be sure to brush the ribs with sauce during the barbecue cooking.

61

SKEWER AND KEBAB COOKING

This age-old method of cooking can still be employed using peeled twigs if you have no skewers available.

It is quick too, as none of the food items used are very large. The skewers on which the food is threaded should be turned frequently to ensure even cooking. You can create kebabs to suit your own taste, using a variety of ingredients, including some with a natural fat content such as bacon, and brushing frequently with a flavored baste. That is all part of the fun, but do remember to wrap kebabs in foil to keep them moist and warm if not to be eaten immediately.

Sausage and Kidney Kebabs (page 64)

SAUSAGE AND KIDNEY KEBABS

Illustrated on page 62

6 lamb kidneys
12 oz. small pork links
1 (15-oz.) can pineapple chunks in natural juice
6 bay leaves

For the baste:

4 tablespoons pineapple juice from the can
3 tablespoons white wine
1 tablespoon clear honey
1 teaspoon dried mixed herbs

Place the kidneys in a bowl and pour boiling water over them. Leave for 1 minute, drain and pour cold water over. Drain again, then skin and quarter the kidneys and snip out the cores. Twist the pork links in half to make about 18 smaller sausages. Drain the pineapple chunks, reserving the juice. Thread the kidney, sausages, pineapple and bay leaves on 6 oiled skewers.

Combine all the ingredients for the baste and use to brush the kebabs. Place on the greased grid. Barbecue for about 20 minutes, turning the skewers frequently and brushing with the baste, until the sausages are cooked. Serve with French bread and **BROWN RICE SALAD** (see page 96). *Serves 6*

BARBECUED BEEF KEFTEDES

1 lb. ground beef
1½ cups fresh bread crumbs
¾ teaspoon salt
finely grated rind of 1 lemon
½ teaspoon dried basil
2 eggs
flour for coating
16 stuffed green olives
olive oil
freshly ground black pepper

Put the beef into a bowl and add the bread crumbs, salt, lemon rind and basil. Mix well then add the eggs and mix again. Divide the mixture into 8 equal portions. Form each into a sausage shape and coat in flour.

Slide 1 olive on each of 8 skewers, then carefully insert the skewers lengthways through the keftedes. Add a second olive to each skewer. Place on a cookie sheet lined with foil and chill for 2 hours.

Brush the loaded skewers with oil and sprinkle with pepper. Barbecue for about 15 minutes, turning frequently. Serve with pita bread and a tomato and onion salad. *Serves 4*

VEGETABLE KEBABS WITH PEANUT AND MUSHROOM SAUCE

3 zucchini, trimmed
4 tablespoons oil
4 tablespoons lemon juice
8 canned baby corn cobs
1 lb. cup mushrooms
8 button onions
2 tomatoes, quartered

For the sauce:

3 tablespoons oil
1 small onion, chopped
2 cups flat mushrooms, chopped
1 (3½-oz.) pack roast salted peanuts
⅔ cup water
3 tablespoons soy sauce
few drops of hot pepper sauce
salt and freshly ground black pepper

Cut the zucchini into 1-inch pieces. Combine the oil and lemon juice in a bowl. Add the corn, zucchini and mushrooms, mix lightly and leave to stand for at least 2 hours, stirring occasionally.

For the sauce, heat the oil in a pan and use to fry the onion and mushrooms for 8 minutes, stirring occasionally. Transfer to a blender or food processor and blend for 30 seconds. Add the peanuts and blend for a further 30 seconds, until fairly smooth. Return the sauce to the pan and stir in the water, soy sauce and hot pepper sauce. Bring to a boil then simmer for 10 minutes. Season with salt and pepper to taste if wished. Keep warm.

Thread the marinated vegetables, onions and tomato wedges on 4 skewers and arrange on the greased grid. Barbecue for about 10 minutes, turning occasionally and brushing with more of the marinade. Hand the peanut and mushroom sauce separately. *Serves 4*

Vegetable Kebabs with Peanut and Mushroom Sauce

SKEWERED SAUSAGE MEATBALLS

1 lb. pork links, skinned
⅔ cup sage and onion stuffing mix
salt and freshly ground black pepper
8 button mushrooms
1 large sweet red pepper, deseeded
8 bay leaves

For the sauce:

1 (14-oz.) can tomatoes
1 tablespoon tomato paste
1 tablespoon Worcestershire sauce
2 teaspoons mild mustard

For the baste:

3 tablespoons dark beer
5 tablespoons oil

For serving:

cooked long grain rice

Combine the sausage meat with the stuffing mix and add salt and pepper if liked. Divide into 12 equal portions and shape each into a ball with floured hands. Trim the stems of the mushrooms level with the caps. Cut the flesh of the pepper into about 12 pieces. Thread the sausage balls on 4 oiled skewers alternating them with the mushrooms, pieces of pepper and bay leaves.

For the sauce, roughly chop the tomatoes and place in a pan with the liquid from the can, the tomato paste, Worcestershire sauce and mustard. Stir until boiling then simmer for 5 minutes. Keep warm on the side of the barbecue while cooking the kebabs.

Mix together the beer and oil and brush over the kebabs. Place on the greased grid. Barbecue for about 30 minutes, brushing frequently with the beer baste and turning half-way through cooking.

Serve the kebabs on a bed of rice on a platter. Hand the sauce separately. *Serves 4*

Skewered Sausage Meatballs

66

Spicy Pork and Fresh Pineapple Kebabs

SPICY PORK AND FRESH PINEAPPLE KEBABS

1¼ lb. boneless lean pork
1 sweet green pepper, deseeded
1 sweet red pepper, deseeded
1 fresh pineapple
1 (scant 1½-oz.) pack Hawaiian flavor spicy
secrets coating for meat
little oil

Cut the pork into 20 cubes. Cut each pepper into 16–20 pieces. Slice the pineapple, halve 3 slices and reserve for the garnish. Remove the rind and any woody core from the remaining slices and divide into 16 chunks.

Put the coating powder into a plastic bag, drop in a few pork cubes, hold the bag closed and shake it until the meat is evenly coated. Remove the coated cubes to a plate and repeat with the remaining pork. Leave the cubes to stand for about 5 minutes, until the surface looks glazed.

Disturbing the coating as little as possible, thread the pork, pineapple chunks and pieces of pepper on 4 oiled skewers. Sprinkle oil lightly over the skewers and place on the greased grid. Barbecue for about 20 minutes, turning occasionally and sprinkling with more oil until the pork is cooked through. Serve on a platter and garnish with the reserved pineapple slices. *Serves 4*

Variation
CHINESE CHICKEN KEBABS Use 1¼ lb. boneless chicken breasts in place of the pork and substitute a Cantonese flavor pack of coating for the Hawaiian flavor. Omit the peppers and pineapple. Drain 8 canned baby corn cobs and 1 (7-oz.) can of bamboo shoots. Cut the shoots into ¼-inch slices. Have ready 8 button mushrooms. When the chicken cubes are well glazed, thread on 4 skewers with the baby corn, bamboo shoots and mushrooms. Sprinkle all ingredients with oil and cook for about the same length of time as for the pork kebabs.

CRISPY CHICKEN
ON STICKS

½ cup finely crushed cornflakes
1 teaspoon curry powder
½ teaspoon salt
1 egg, beaten
1 sweet red pepper, deseeded
2 boneless chicken breasts, skinned
½ cup halved button mushrooms

Mix together the cornflake crumbs, curry powder and salt in a bowl. Place the egg in a shallow dish. Thickly slice the pepper flesh, then cut into 1-inch strips.

Cut the chicken flesh into cubes, approximately 1 inch in size. Dip the cubes in egg and toss them in the cornflake mixture, pressing it on well.

Thread the coated chicken cubes, pepper strips and mushroom halves on about 8 wooden sticks or skewers. Place on a cookie sheet lined with foil and chill for 2 hours.

Arrange the chicken sticks on the greased grid. Barbecue for about 20 minutes, turning frequently. Serve with pita breads and salad. *Serves 4*

CHICKEN AND MANGO
KEBABS WITH NUT RICE

3 boneless chicken breasts, skinned
juice of 2 limes
5 tablespoons olive oil
3 tablespoons chopped mint
1 teaspoon light brown sugar
1 large ripe mango
extra olive oil
salt and freshly ground black pepper

For the nut rice:

¼ teaspoon ground turmeric
2½ cups chicken bouillon
few drops of yellow food coloring (optional)
generous 1 cup long grain rice
2 tablespoons butter
1 tablespoon oil
⅓ cup blanched almonds

Cut the chicken into even-sized cubes. Mix together the lime juice, oil, mint and sugar and stir in the chicken cubes until evenly coated. Cover and chill for 2 hours.

Meanwhile cook the nut rice. Place the turmeric and stock in a pan and stir well. Add a few drops of coloring if wished, then sprinkle in the rice and bring to a boil. Stir once, cover and simmer for 15 minutes, or until the rice is tender and has absorbed the stock.

Heat the butter and oil in a pan and use to fry the almonds until golden brown. Fork the almonds and buttery juices into the cooked rice and season with salt and pepper to taste. Keep warm in the covered pan on the side of the barbecue while the kebabs are cooking.

Pit the mango and cut the flesh into chunks about the same size as the chicken. Thread the chicken and mango cubes on 4 greased skewers. Brush with the marinade and sprinkle with a little extra oil and salt and pepper.

Place the kebabs on the greased grid. Barbecue for 10 minutes then turn, brush again with marinade and sprinkle with seasoning. Barbecue for a further 8–10 minutes, or until cooked through.

Arrange the warm nut rice on a serving dish and lay the kebabs on top. *Serves 4*

LAMB SKEWERS
WITH ROSEMARY

1 lb. lean lamb, cubed
5 tablespoons clear honey
3 tablespoons oil
finely grated rind and juice of ½ lemon
1 tablespoon chopped fresh parsley
½ teaspoon dried rosemary
¼ teaspoon freshly ground black pepper
1 medium-sized onion, quartered
salt

Put the meat cubes in a shallow dish. Combine the honey, oil, lemon rind and juice, parsley, rosemary and pepper, and spoon evenly over the lamb. Cover and leave to stand for at least 8 hours, turning the cubes occasionally.

Carefully separate the onion into layers. Thread cubes of lamb and single pieces of onion alternately on 4 greased skewers.

Place the skewers on the greased grid. Barbecue for about 20 minutes, turning the kebabs occasionally and basting with the remaining marinade, until cooked through. Sprinkle with salt and serve garnished with lemon slices and parsley sprigs. *Serves 4*

Crispy Chicken on Sticks, Herby Chicken Fingers (page 44)

MUSTARD BEEF KEBABS

Mustard Beef Kebabs

1½ lb. rump steak
3 zucchini, trimmed
1 large sweet red pepper, deseeded

For the baste:

4 tablespoons mild mustard
1 tablespoon creamed horseradish sauce
3 tablespoons oil
salt and freshly ground black pepper

Trim the steak and cut into 1-inch cubes. Cut each zucchini into 4 chunks. Cut the pepper flesh into 12 pieces. Thread the steak, zucchini and red pepper alternately on to 6 greased skewers.

Combine the mustard, horseradish sauce and oil and season with salt and pepper to taste. Brush this mixture over the kebabs and place on the greased grid. Barbecue for about 15 minutes, turning and brushing frequently with more of the baste until cooked through. Serve with rolls and a salad. *Serves 6*

Variation
APPLE MUSTARD PORK KEBABS Substitute pork tenderloin for the rump steak and use 3 tablespoons applesauce instead of the horseradish sauce.

FRUITY TANDOORI LAMB SKEWERS

1¼ lb. boneless lean lamb, cubed
1 (6½-oz.) jar cranberry orange sauce
⅔ cup plain yogurt
1 teaspoon curry powder
2 cloves of garlic, finely chopped
1 large onion, cut into wedges
oil

For serving:

cooked long-grain rice

Prick the cubes of meat all over with a fork and place in a shallow dish.

Put the cranberry orange sauce in a food processor or blender with the yogurt, curry powder and garlic, and blend until the ingredients are well combined. Spread this paste over the meat cubes, cover and leave to stand for about 8 hours.

Thread the meat cubes and wedges of onion on 4 skewers, brush with oil and place on the greased grid. Barbecue for about 20 minutes, turning frequently and brushing with more oil during cooking. Arrange a bed of fluffy rice on a platter and lay the cooked skewers on top. Serve with a lettuce and cucumber salad. *Serves 4*

BACON BITES WITH SPICY DIP

12 slices Canadian style bacon
⅔ cup finely chopped cooked chicken
1 cup fresh bread crumbs
½ teaspoon chopped fresh parsley
salt and freshly ground black pepper
little beaten egg

For the dip:

1 tablespoon butter, melted
1 small onion, finely chopped
5 tablespoons tomato catsup
1 teaspoon light brown sugar
1 tablespoon Worcestershire sauce
2 teaspoons white wine vinegar
¼ teaspoon hot mustard
1 tablespoon mango chutney, chopped

Lay out the bacon slices on a board. Place the chicken, bread crumbs and parsley in a bowl and season with salt and pepper to taste. Mix well. Add just enough egg to bind the mixture together.

Place a little of the chicken filling on the narrowest end of each bacon slice and roll up neatly to enclose the filling. Thread the rolls carefully on to oiled skewers.

Mix together all the ingredients for the dip, place in a dish and set this in the center of a serving plate. Line the plate with lettuce leaves.

Place the bacon bites on the greased grid. Barbecue for about 8 minutes, turning frequently, until the bacon is crisp. When they are cooked, remove from the skewers and arrange on the lettuce leaves for serving. *Serves 6*

CHICKEN AND PINEAPPLE KEBABS

1 (15-oz.) can pineapple chunks
4 tablespoons soy sauce
2 teaspoons ground ginger
1 clove of garlic, finely chopped
1 teaspoon dry mustard powder
3 tablespoons clear honey
5 tablespoons dry vermouth
1½ lb. boneless chicken breasts
sweet paprika

Drain the pineapple chunks and measure ½ cup of the syrup into a pan. Add the soy sauce, ginger, garlic, mustard powder, honey and vermouth and heat gently, stirring until blended.

Cut the chicken breasts into 24 cubes and place in a shallow dish. Pour over the vermouth mixture, cover and chill for at least 2 hours.

Thread the chicken cubes and pineapple chunks alternately on 4 oiled skewers. Brush with marinade, sprinkle lightly with paprika and place on the greased grid. Barbecue for about 20 minutes, turning frequently and brushing with more marinade until the chicken is cooked through and turning brown. Serve with WALNUT RICE SALAD (see page 96). *Serves 4*

LAMB AND KIDNEY KEBABS

Illustrated on page 2

1 lb. boneless leg of lamb
4 lamb kidneys, halved
1 sweet green pepper, deseeded
1 cup button mushrooms
bay leaves
4 tomatoes, quartered
salt and freshly ground black pepper

For the marinade:

3 tablespoons oil
1 tablespoon vinegar
1 clove of garlic, crushed
1 medium-sized onion, roughly chopped

Cut the lamb into cubes and place in a shallow dish. Combine all the ingredients for the marinade and pour over the lamb. Marinate for about 8 hours.

Skin the kidneys and snip out the cores. Cut the pepper flesh into pieces and blanch these in boiling salted water for 2 minutes. Drain well. Trim the stems on the mushrooms level with the caps.

Drain the lamb cubes. Thread on 4 large or 8 smaller oiled skewers, alternating with mushrooms, bay leaves, pieces of kidney, tomato and green pepper.

Brush the kebabs with marinade, sprinkle with salt and pepper to taste and place on the greased grid. Barbecue for about 20 minutes, turning and brushing with more of the marinade. *Serves 8*

WAIKIKI KEBABS

2 thick slices smoked shoulder, total weight
about 1½ lb.
1 sweet green pepper, deseeded
1 medium-sized onion
2 slices fresh or canned pineapple

For the marinade:

3 tablespoons Worcestershire sauce
2 teaspoons mild mustard
juice of 1 lemon
1 tablespoon tomato paste
4 tablespoons oil
salt and freshly ground black pepper

For serving:

cooked long grain rice

Soak the shoulder slices in cold water for 4 hours. Drain and cut into neat cubes. Place in a pan, cover with fresh cold water and bring to a boil. Simmer for 20 minutes, then drain.

For the marinade, mix together in a large bowl the Worcestershire sauce, mustard, lemon juice, tomato paste and oil and season with salt and pepper to taste. Stir in the meat cubes while they are still warm. Leave to stand for 30 minutes.

Cut the pepper flesh and onion into chunks and divide each pineapple slice into 6 pieces. Thread the meat cubes, pepper, onion and pineapple on 2 large or 4 smaller greased skewers and brush with some of the remaining marinade.

Place the kebabs on the greased grid. Barbecue for about 15 minutes, turning frequently and brushing with more marinade during cooking, until browned. Arrange a bed of rice on a serving dish and lay the cooked kebabs on top. *Serves 4*

PICKLED ONION KEBABS

2 eating apples
2 lamb kidneys
4 oz. lamb liver
8 button mushrooms
8 bacon slices
8 pickled onions
5 tablespoons bottled barbecue sauce

Core and quarter the apples, removing the peel if preferred. Pour boiling water over the kidneys, drain, cover with cold water and drain again. Skin the kidneys, quarter and snip out the cores. Cut the liver into cubes about 1 inch in size. Trim the stems of the mushrooms level with the caps. Roll up each bacon slice.

Load 4 skewers with bacon rolls, apple wedges, liver cubes, pickled onions and pieces of kidney. Brush with barbecue sauce and place on the greased grid. Barbecue for about 20 minutes, turning frequently and brushing with more sauce, until cooked to taste. Serve with a tomato salad and wholewheat rolls. *Serves 4*

BEEF BROCHETTES WITH YOGURT MARINADE

1½ lb. rump steak, cubed
1 sweet green pepper, deseeded

For the marinade:

⅔ cup plain yogurt
½ teaspoon ground coriander
½ teaspoon ground cumin
1 clove of garlic, finely chopped
3 tablespoons lemon juice
1 teaspoon salt

For the sauce:

2 tablespoons block margarine
1 large onion, chopped
1 tablespoon tomato paste
3 tablespoons wine vinegar
3 tablespoons Worcestershire sauce
3 tablespoons brown sugar
2 teaspoons dry mustard powder
1¼ cups applejack

Trim the steak, cut into 1-inch cubes and place in a shallow dish.

Combine the marinade ingredients and pour over the steak cubes. Cover and leave to stand for at least 1 hour, stirring occasionally.

Meanwhile, make the sauce. Melt the margarine in a pan and use to fry the onion until soft. Add the tomato paste, vinegar, Worcestershire sauce, sugar and mustard powder and stir well. Blend in

Waikiki Kebabs

the applejack and bring to a boil, stirring. Simmer for 10 minutes, until slightly thickened.

Cut the pepper flesh into squares. Remove the steak cubes from the marinade and thread on 4 long skewers, alternating with pieces of pepper. Keep the ingredients close together.
Brush the kebabs with any remaining marinade and arrange on the greased grid. Barbecue for 15–20 minutes, turning frequently, until the steak is done to taste. Serve with fluffy cooked rice and hand the barbecue sauce separately. *Serves 4*

Wanaka Barbecued Lamb Spareribs

SAUCY LIVER AND KIDNEY KEBABS

$\frac{1}{2}$ sweet green pepper, deseeded
8 oz. lamb liver
3 lamb kidneys
2 medium-sized onions, quartered
4 bay leaves
1 (8-oz.) can apricot halves, drained

For the sauce:

$\frac{2}{3}$ cup orange juice
3 tablespoons lemon juice
1 tablespoon clear honey
1 tablespoon tomato paste
$\frac{1}{4}$ teaspoon ground ginger
$\frac{1}{2}$ teaspoon Lo Salt (low sodium salt)
1 tablespoon cornstarch
3 tablespoons syrup from can of apricots

Cut the green pepper into squares and the liver into $\frac{3}{4}$-inch cubes. Pour boiling water over the kidneys, drain and cover with cold water. Drain again and remove the skins. Quarter the kidneys and snip out the cores. Thread the liver, kidney, onion, bay leaves, pepper squares and apricot halves on 4 skewers.

For the sauce, mix together the fruit juices, honey, tomato paste, ginger and low sodium salt in

a pan. Brush this mixture over the loaded skewers and arrange on the greased grid. Barbecue for 20 minutes, turning frequently.

Blend the cornstarch with the apricot syrup, add to the remaining sauce and bring to a boil on the barbecue, stirring until thickened. Serve the kebabs and sauce with rice and a salad. *Serves 4*

WELLINGTON LAMB KEBABS

Illustrated on page 6

1 lb. boneless lean lamb
1 tablespoon oil
1 tablespoon wine vinegar
$\frac{1}{4}$ teaspoon dried basil
salt and freshly ground black pepper
1 small sweet green pepper, deseeded
1 small sweet red pepper, deseeded
2 small onions, quartered

Cut the lamb into 16 cubes and place in a shallow dish. Mix together the oil, vinegar, basil and a little salt and pepper. Pour over the lamb, cover and leave to stand for at least 8 hours.

74

Meanwhile, cut the pepper flesh into squares. Drain the lamb cubes and thread them on 4 oiled skewers, alternating with the pepper and onion.

Place the kebabs on the greased grid. Barbecue for about 20 minutes, turning frequently and brushing with more of the marinade. *Serves 4*

WANAKA BARBECUED LAMB SPARERIBS

2 breasts of lamb
⅔ cup plum jam
5 tablespoons tomato catsup
1 tablespoon Worcestershire sauce
1 tablespoon mild mustard

Using a pair of scissors or a sharp knife, cut the breasts of lamb between the bones. Put the ribs in a large pan and cover with cold water. Boil steadily for 20 minutes, then drain.

Meanwhile, mix together the jam, catsup, Worcestershire sauce and mustard in a large bowl. Add the ribs while they are still hot and stir well to coat thoroughly. Cover and leave to stand for 2 hours if time permits, although the ribs can be cooked at once if necessary.

Thread the ribs on pairs of long greased skewers held 2 inches apart so that they are easy to turn during cooking. Place on the greased grid. Barbecue for about 20 minutes, turning frequently and brushing with any remaining marinade. Serve with a mixed salad and crusty rolls. *Serves 6*

STEAK AND KIDNEY SKEWERS

3 lamb kidneys
1 lb. lean rump or sirloin steak, cubed
2 medium-sized onions, quartered
1 cup button mushrooms
6 tomatoes, halved

For the marinade:

3 tablespoons malt vinegar
3 tablespoons oil
1 clove of garlic, finely chopped
¼ teaspoon dried mixed herbs
finely grated rind of ¼ lemon
salt and freshly ground black pepper

Pour boiling water over the kidneys, drain, cover with cold water and drain again. Remove the skin, quarter the kidneys and snip out the cores.

Mix together the vinegar, oil, garlic, herbs, lemon rind and a little salt and pepper in a plastic food bag. Add the steak and kidney, close the bag with a twist-tie and turn it so that the meat is coated with marinade. Leave to stand for at least 2 hours.

Thread the steak, kidney, onion, mushrooms and tomato halves on 6 skewers and arrange on the greased grid. Barbecue for about 20 minutes, turning frequently and brushing with more of the marinade, until done to taste. Serve with coleslaw and potatoes baked in their skins. *Serves 6*

PORK KEBABS WITH PITA POCKETS

1½ lb. pork tenderloin
⅔ cup plain yogurt
3 tablespoons sage and onion mustard
1 tablespoon brown sugar
salt and freshly ground black pepper

For serving:

pita bread

Cut the pork into small cubes. Place in a shallow container. Combine the yogurt, mustard and brown sugar, spoon over the pork and mix well. Cover and leave to stand for at least 8 hours.

Thread the pork cubes on 8 greased wooden skewers, season lightly with salt and pepper and place on the greased grid. Barbecue for about 20 minutes, turning frequently and basting with more of the marinade, until cooked through.

Serve with pita bread, a mixed salad and extra mustard. *Serves 8*

Variations
CHICKEN AND CHIVE MUSTARD KEBABS Substitute boneless chicken breast for the pork tenderloin and use chive mustard instead of the sage and onion mustard. Barbecuing time will be about the same.
LAMB AND TARRAGON MUSTARD KEBABS Substitute boneless lean leg of lamb for the pork tenderloin and use tarragon and thyme mustard instead of the sage and onion mustard. Barbecuing time will be about the same.

BANANA AND BACON KEBABS WITH CURRY SAUCE

8 slices Canadian style bacon plus 8 bacon
strips
1 small sweet red pepper, deseeded
1 small sweet green pepper, deseeded
2 medium-sized onions, quartered
2 bananas
$\frac{1}{4}$ cup butter, melted

For the sauce:

2 tablespoons butter
2 teaspoons curry powder
1 tablespoon flour
$\frac{2}{3}$ cup chicken bouillon
3 tablespoons light cream

Roll up each piece of bacon to make 16 rolls. Cut the pepper flesh into squares. Blanch the onion and pepper squares in boiling water for 2 minutes, then drain.

For the sauce, melt the butter in a small pan and stir in the curry powder and flour. Cook for 1 minute, stirring, then blend in the stock and stir until boiling. Simmer for 2 minutes, cool slightly and stir in the cream. Transfer to a serving jug and keep warm.

Cut the bananas into $\frac{1}{2}$-inch slices. Thread the bacon rolls, pepper squares, onion pieces and banana slices evenly on 4 oiled skewers. Brush with the melted butter and place on the greased grid. Barbecue for about 16 minutes, turning occasionally and brushing with the remaining butter, until the bacon is golden. Arrange on a platter and serve with the sauce and a mixed salad. *Serves 4*

Variation

APRICOT AND BACON KEBABS Use 12 drained canned apricot halves in place of the banana slices and add 3 tablespoons of the syrup from the can to the melted butter for brushing the kebabs during cooking.

EAST INDIAN SATAY

$1\frac{1}{2}$ teaspoons ground coriander
$\frac{1}{2}$ teaspoon salt
1 medium-sized onion, chopped
1 clove of garlic, chopped
3 tablespoons soy sauce
1 tablespoon lemon juice
$\frac{1}{2}$ cup roast salted peanuts, ground
2 tablespoons light brown sugar
4 tablespoons peanut or salad oil
freshly ground black pepper
$1\frac{1}{2}$ lb. boneless chicken breasts, cubed
1-inch squares of sweet pepper, if possible red,
green and yellow

For serving:

chicory leaves

Combine the coriander, salt, onion, garlic, soy sauce, lemon juice, peanuts, sugar and oil in a food processor or blender until smooth. Add pepper to taste.

Put the chicken cubes in a shallow dish, pour over the peanut mixture and stir lightly. Cover and leave to stand for about 4 hours, turning the ingredients occasionally.

Thread the chicken cubes on 4 greased skewers, alternating them with squares of pepper. Place on the greased grid. Barbecue over high heat for about 20 minutes, turning the kebabs frequently and brushing with more of the marinade during cooking, until brown but not dry.

Line a serving dish with chicory leaves, lay the kebabs on top and hand SOUR CREAM AND PEANUT DIP separately. *Serves 4*

Accompaniment

SOUR CREAM AND PEANUT DIP Mix together $\frac{2}{3}$ cup sour cream and $\frac{2}{3}$ cup plain yogurt. Chop 2 scallions, finely chop 1 clove of garlic and chop $\frac{1}{3}$ cup dry roasted peanuts. Stir almost all these into the yogurt mixture, transfer to a bowl and sprinkle the rest on top. Serve with the satay.

East Indian Satay

SKEWERED SAUSAGES

2¼ lb. pork and beef links
4 mild onions, cut into wedges
16 miniature pickled cucumbers

For the sauce:

1 (8-oz.) can tomatoes
⅓ cup cider or tarragon vinegar
3 tablespoons Worcestershire sauce
2 small bay leaves
1 clove of garlic, finely chopped
4 tablespoons finely chopped onion
3 stalks of celery, finely chopped
½ lemon, quartered
1 tablespoon brown sugar
1¼ cups apple juice
salt and freshly ground black pepper

For the sauce, roughly chop the tomatoes and place in a pan with the liquid from the can and remaining sauce ingredients. Bring to a boil, stirring, then simmer for 30 minutes. Remove the bay leaves and lemon pieces and season with salt and pepper to taste if wished.

Load 8 skewers with sausages, wedges of onion and pickled cucumbers, threading the skewers lengthways through the sausages.

Brush the sausages and other ingredients with sauce and place on the greased grid. Barbecue for 15 minutes, turning the skewers frequently. Serve with the remaining sauce and HOT GARLIC AND HERB BREAD (see page 104). *Serves 8*

MUSTARDY HAM KEBABS

1½ lb smoked ham in 2 thick slices
2 cooked corn cobs
2 cups mushrooms

For the marinade:

1–2 tablespoons mild burger mustard
1 tablespoon lemon juice
3 tablespoons oil

For the sauce:

4 tablespoons mild burger mustard
3 tablespoons chopped parsley

Cube the ham, cut the corn cobs into 1-inch pieces and trim the stems on the mushrooms level with the caps. Thread these ingredients on 6 oiled skewers. Lay the loaded skewers in a shallow dish.

For the marinade, mix together all the ingredients and spoon evenly over the kebabs. Cover and chill for 2 hours, turning the kebabs once during this time. Meanwhile for the sauce, combine the mustard and parsley.

Place the kebabs on the greased grid. Barbecue for about 20 minutes, turning them frequently and basting with any remaining marinade. Arrange on a platter, spoon the sauce over the kebabs and serve garnished with parsley sprigs. *Serves 6*

BARBECUED FISH KEBABS

4 whole mackerel or herring, cleaned
3 small onions, quartered
4 tomatoes, halved

For the sauce:

1¼ cups chicken or fish bouillon
⅔ cup tomato catsup
3 tablespoons Worcestershire sauce
3 tablespoons wine vinegar
3 tablespoons brown sugar
2 drops of hot pepper sauce
3 tablespoons tomato paste
1 tablespoon cornstarch
salt and freshly ground black pepper

For serving:

cooked long grain rice

Trim the fish then open out on a board with the skin side upwards and press along the backbones. Remove the bones. Reshape the fish and cut each across into 4 pieces.

For the sauce, mix together all the ingredients, except the seasoning, in a pan and stir until boiling. Add salt and pepper to taste. Keep the sauce warm in the pan on the side of the barbecue.

Thread the fish on 4 oiled skewers alternating with pieces of onion and tomato halves. Place on the greased grid. Barbecue for 10 minutes, turning the skewers frequently and brushing them with a little of the sauce during cooking.

Lay the skewers on a bed of rice and hand the sauce separately. *Serves 4*

Barbecued Fish Kebabs

SPIT-ROASTING AND PARCEL COOKING

Spit-roasting imparts a delicious flavor
to meat or poultry. That's because the savory juices
roll round the joint as it turns, impregnating
the flesh, rather than dripping off into
a pan set beneath it, or into the fire itself.
Prepare meats that might toughen in
cooking, by putting them beforehand into
a flavorsome marinade. This can later be used as
a baste during spit-roasting and any left
over can be served as a sauce with the meat.
If you prefer, spoon the remaining marinade into
baked potatoes or other accompaniments
such as pasta or rice.
Smaller items, that might dry out too much if open
broiled or roasted, cook to perfection when enclosed in
foil parcels. A tasty blend of vegetables can be
gathered in a foil "cup" and sealed to cook together.

Italian Fish Bake (page 88)

MOROCCAN ROTISSERIE CHICKEN

1 (3½-lb.) chicken

For the baste:

3 tablespoons oil
3 tablespoons lemon juice
½ teaspoon ground turmeric
½ teaspoon ground cardamom
½ teaspoon ground cinnamon
pinch of ground allspice
1 teaspoon salt
¼ teaspoon pepper

For the garnish:

sprigs of watercress
lemon wedges

Thread the chicken on the spit and secure the clamps. Combine all the ingredients for the baste. Brush the chicken with this mixture and leave to stand for 1 hour.

Spit-roast for about 1¼ hours, brushing occasionally with the rest of the baste during cooking, until the chicken juices run clear when tested, or when a meat thermometer inserted into the thickest part of the thigh registers 190°F.

Remove the chicken from the spit, leave to stand for 5 minutes then divide into quarters. Garnish each portion with watercress sprigs and wedges of lemon. Serve with cooked rice and a tomato and black olive salad. *Serves 4*

SPIT-ROAST GINGERED TURKEY ROLL

2¼ lb. turkey breast roll

For the baste:

3 tablespoons oil
⅓ cup soy sauce
3 tablespoons clear honey
1 tablespoon red wine vinegar
1 teaspoon ground ginger
1 clove of garlic, very finely chopped

Defrost the turkey roll and remove the plastic casing. Combine all the ingredients for the baste. Brush the turkey roll with this mixture and leave to stand for 30 minutes.

Thread the turkey roll on the spit and secure the clamps. Spit-roast for about 1 hour, brushing with the remaining ginger baste during this time, or until the turkey juices run clear when tested. If using a meat thermometer, this should register 190°F when the turkey is ready.

Push the roll off the spit and leave to stand for 5 minutes before cutting into thick slices. Serve with Barbecued Potato Slices (see page 104) and a radish and beansprout salad. *Serves 6*

SPIT-ROAST LAMB WITH BEANS

generous 1 cup dried navy beans
salt and freshly ground black pepper
2 bay leaves
3 tablespoons oil
1 large onion, sliced
1 clove of garlic, finely chopped
3 tablespoons chopped mixed herbs
1 (4-lb.) leg or shoulder of lamb, boned, rolled
and tied

For the glaze:

½ cup red currant jelly
5 tablespoons bottled barbecue sauce

Soak the beans in plenty of cold water overnight. Drain well, place in a pan with fresh water to cover and bring to a boil. Skim the surface, season with salt and pepper to taste and add the bay leaves. Bring to a boil, cover and simmer for 30 minutes.

Heat the oil and use to fry the onion and garlic lightly until beginning to soften. Stir into the bean mixture, cover and continue cooking for a further 20 minutes, or until the beans are tender but not breaking up. Drain off any excess liquid, adjust the seasoning if necessary and stir in the herbs. Transfer to another pan or a dish and keep warm on the side of the barbecue.

Rub the meat with salt and pepper and place on the spit, over a drip pan. Barbecue for 25–30 minutes per 1 lb. or until a meat thermometer inserted into the deepest part of the meat registers 190°F.

Meanwhile, very gently melt the red currant jelly and barbecue sauce together in a small pan. Use this mixture to baste the lamb during the last 30 minutes of cooking time. Serve the lamb with the beans, and baked potatoes and tomatoes if liked. *Serves 8*

Spit-Roast Lamb with Beans

Spit-Roast Turkey with Spiced Apple, Barbecued Fruit Salad (page 110)

SPIT-ROAST TURKEY WITH SPICED APPLE

1 (8–10-lb.) deep basted turkey
2 large tart apples, peeled
$\frac{2}{3}$ cup apple juice
3 tablespoons light brown sugar
$\frac{1}{2}$ teaspoon ground allspice

Ensure that the turkey is completely defrosted, then remove the giblets. Core and roughly chop the apples and use to fill the cavity of the bird. Position on the spit and fit the clamps tightly.

Spit-roast the turkey for 20 minutes per 1 lb. or until a meat thermometer inserted into the thickest part of the thigh registers 190°F. After the first hour of cooking, brush the skin of the turkey frequently with apple juice.

When the bird is cooked, scoop the apple filling into a bowl. Beat well until smooth with the sugar and spice. Transfer to a serving dish. *Serves 8*

Variation
KETTLE-ROAST TURKEY Fill the turkey with apple as above. Divide the bed of coals, banking them on each side of a drip pan. Place a lightly greased grid about 4 inches above the drip pan, set the turkey on this, breast side upwards, taking care that it is directly over the drip pan. Cover the barbecue and adjust the vents as directed. Roast the turkey for 15 minutes per 1 lb. or until the meat thermometer registers 190°F, basting with apple juice as before.

LAMB STEAKS WITH FRUIT SIDE DISH

Illustrated on page 6

4 lamb leg bone steaks or chops
1 (15-oz.) can sliced kiwi fruit
2 teaspoons curry powder
1 medium-sized onion, finely chopped
3 tablespoons vinegar
1 tablespoon oil
1 tablespoon light brown sugar
pinch of ground cinnamon
1 orange
1 red-skinned dessert apple
2 cups shredded white cabbage
3 tablespoons toasted slivered almonds
1 tablespoon Italian dressing

Put the lamb in a shallow dish. Drain the syrup from the kiwi fruit, take 5 tablespoons of the syrup and mix with the curry powder, onion, vinegar, oil, sugar and cinnamon. Pour over the lamb, cover and leave to stand for at least 4 hours.

To make the side dish, peel the orange and divide into slices, discarding any membrane and pith. Cut each slice in half. Core and slice the apple. Combine the cabbage with the apple, orange, kiwi fruit slices and almonds in a bowl. Stir together 1 tablespoon of the remaining kiwi fruit syrup and the dressing, pour over the ingredients and toss.

Drain the lamb steaks. Enclose each one in a foil parcel. Arrange the foil parcels on the grid. Barbecue for about 30 minutes. Unwrap, arrange on the greased grid and barbecue for 5 minutes, turning once. Serve with the remaining marinade and the side dish. *Serves 4*

SPIT-ROAST DUCKLINGS WITH APRICOT GLAZE

Illustrated on page 122

2 (4$\frac{1}{2}$-lb.) ducklings
salt
$\frac{2}{3}$ cup apricot jam (sieved if preferred)
$\frac{2}{3}$ cup white vermouth

Defrost ducklings if necessary. Remove the giblets and pat dry inside and out.

Sprinkle the ducks with salt and truss if necessary. Position on the spit and fit the clamps. Set over a drip pan. Spit-roast for 30 minutes.

Combine the apricot jam and vermouth in a pan and stir until blended. Brush the ducks with this mixture and continue cooking for a further 1–1$\frac{1}{2}$ hours, basting frequently with more mixture, until juices from the thigh run clear when tested with a skewer. Remove the ducklings from the spit to a serving dish and spoon any remaining baste over the top. Serve with HERBY STUFFED TOMATOES (page 123) and mixed rice and peas. *Serves 8*

Variation
GLAZED DUCKLING PORTIONS Use the apricot glaze from the main recipe to brush 8 duck portions arranged on a greased grid. Allow 40 minutes cooking for breast portions and 50 minutes for leg portions, turning and brushing frequently with the glaze after the first 20 minutes. This quantity of glaze will coat 8 duck portions.

CRAB-STUFFED TURKEY BREASTS

Crab-Stuffed Turkey Breasts, Prawnie or Shrimp and Pasta Salad (page 95)

6 turkey breast fillets
8 oz. crab sticks, chopped
$\frac{1}{3}$ cup butter, softened
$\frac{1}{4}$ teaspoon ground nutmeg
salt and freshly ground black pepper

For the coating:

$\frac{1}{4}$ cup all-purpose flour
1 teaspoon sweet paprika pepper
2 tablespoons butter, melted

Cut a pocket in each turkey fillet with a sharp knife. Mix together the crab sticks, butter and nutmeg and season with salt and pepper to taste. Use this mixture to fill the turkey fillet cavities.

Combine the flour and paprika. Brush the stuffed fillets with butter, then coat them in the paprika flour. Enclose in foil parcels and place on the grid. Barbecue for about 30 minutes. Unwrap and place on the greased grid for 5 minutes, turning once, until well browned. *Serves 6*

BACON-STUFFED EGGPLANTS

2 large eggplants
salt and freshly ground black pepper
3 tablespoons butter
4 slices Canadian style bacon, chopped
1 medium-sized onion, finely chopped
2 large tomatoes, chopped
2 teaspoons chopped thyme
2 teaspoons chopped parsley

Cut the eggplants in half lengthways, scoop out the flesh and chop roughly. Sprinkle the eggplant shells and the chopped flesh with salt and leave to stand for 20 minutes. Rinse well then drain.

Melt the butter in a pan, stir in the chopped eggplant, bacon and onion and cook for 5 minutes, stirring occasionally. Mix in the tomato and herbs and season with salt and pepper to taste. Pile the mixture into the eggplant shells.

Enclose each stuffed eggplant half in a square of foil, shiny side inwards, crimping the edges well together to make airtight parcels. Place the foil parcels on the grid. Barbecue for about 20 minutes, or until the eggplants feel tender when pressed. Fold back the foil to make boat-shaped containers for serving. *Serves 4*

FRENCH PEAS Quarter 3 lettuce hearts and trim and finely chop 4 scallions. Place the lettuce and scallions in a bowl, add 1 lb. frozen peas and 1 tablespoon chopped mint and mix well. Line 4 fruit dishes with foil, to make neat shapes. Divide the pea mixture among them and dot with butter. Fold up the foil and crimp the edges to make airtight parcels. Place the shaped foil parcels on the grid. Barbecue for about 10 minutes, turning the parcels over half-way through cooking. *Serves 4–6*

CORN AND PINEAPPLE PARCELS Combine $1\frac{1}{3}$ cups drained canned corn kernels with $\frac{1}{3}$ cup chopped canned pineapple. Divide among 2 sheets of foil, sprinkle with salt, pepper and pineapple syrup from the can and dot with butter. Fold up the foil and seal the edges to make airtight parcels. Barbecue for about 10 minutes, until piping hot. *Serves 4*

Bacon-Stuffed Eggplants, French Peas, Corn and Pineapple Parcels

87

ITALIAN FISH BAKE

Illustrated on page 80

4 (8–10-oz.) red or grey mullet or snappers, cleaned
salt and freshly ground black pepper
1 small sweet red pepper, deseeded
1 small sweet green pepper, deseeded
12 oz. zucchini, trimmed
1 medium-sized onion, sliced
1 cup button mushrooms, sliced
1 clove of garlic, finely chopped
2 tablespoons butter or margarine

Trim off the fish fins, then wash and dry.

Have ready 4 sheets of foil, each large enough to enclose a fish plus vegetables, and grease lightly. Lay a fish on each sheet and season with salt and pepper to taste. Slice the pepper flesh, and thinly slice the zucchini. Arrange all the vegetables and garlic around the fish and dot with the butter.

Fold up the foil to make airtight parcels and arrange on the grid. Barbecue for about 30 minutes, or until the fish and vegetables are cooked. Accompany with a new potato salad. *Serves 4*

SIMPLE BARBECUED SALMON STEAKS

1 tablespoon butter, melted
3 tablespoons oil
salt and freshly ground black pepper
1 teaspoon lemon juice
4 (6-oz.) salmon steaks

Warm together the butter and oil until the butter melts, then season well with salt and pepper to taste. Add the lemon juice.

Brush the salmon steaks with the butter mixture. Enclose in foil parcels and arrange on the grid. Barbecue for 7 minutes on each side, or until the salmon flesh separates into flakes when tested with a fork. *Serves 4*

Variations
LIME BASTED SALMON STEAKS Very finely grate the rind and squeeze the juice from $\frac{1}{2}$ lime. Cut the remaining lime half into very thin wedges. Use 1 teaspoon of the lime juice and all the grated rind in the baste in place of the lemon juice. Barbecue the steaks as in the main recipe and serve garnished with the lime wedges.

SALMON STEAKS WITH FLAMBÉED PINEAPPLE Barbecue the salmon steaks as in the main recipe. Meanwhile, brush 4 drained canned pineapple slices with any remaining baste or with oil and barbecue for 3 minutes on each side. Transfer the salmon steaks to a serving platter away from the barbecue, top each with a hot pineapple slice and spoon 1 teaspoon brandy over each topped steak. Ignite and serve immediately, before the flames die down. It is essential that the salmon and pineapple are both hot for this method to work successfully.

OTAK OTAK

$\frac{2}{3}$ cup shredded coconut
$\frac{2}{3}$ cup boiling water
6–8 dried red chili peppers, crushed
1 medium-sized onion, very finely chopped
$\frac{1}{2}$ cup roast salted peanuts, very finely chopped
finely grated rind of $\frac{1}{2}$ lemon
8 basil leaves, chopped, or 1 teaspoon dried basil
1 egg, beaten
$\frac{1}{2}$ teaspoon ground turmeric
salt and freshly ground black pepper
8 (6-oz.) cod steaks

For the garnish:

sprigs of coriander or parsley

For serving:

lemon wedges

First make the coconut milk. Put the coconut in a bowl and pour on the boiling water. Leave to stand until cool then strain, pressing the coconut shreds to extract as much liquid as possible. Reserve the coconut "milk" and discard the coconut.

Mix together the crushed chili, onion, peanuts, lemon rind and basil in a bowl. Stir in the coconut milk, egg and turmeric and season with salt and pepper to taste.

Have ready 8 sheets of foil, each large enough to enclose a fish steak loosely. Place a cod steak on each sheet and spoon the chili mixture on top. Fold up the foil and crimp the edges together to make the airtight parcels.

Arrange the foil parcels on the grid. Barbecue for about 20 minutes, or until the fish flakes easily when tested with a fork. Transfer the steaks and topping to a serving dish and garnish with herbs. Hand lemon wedges separately. *Serves 8*

FISH TERIYAKI

1 (2–3-lb.) piece of cod or haddock
4 tablespoons soy sauce
$\frac{1}{3}$ cup dry sherry
3 tablespoons lemon juice
$\frac{1}{2}$ teaspoon ground ginger

Otak Otak

Cut the piece of fish lengthways into 2 fillets and lift off the bones. Lay each piece of fish, skin side downwards, on a sheet of foil. Slash the flesh side of each fillet several times with a sharp knife.

Put the soy sauce, sherry, lemon juice and ginger in a small pan and bring to a boil, stirring. Spoon the sherry mixture over the flesh of the fish. Fold up the foil and enclose each fillet loosely in an airtight parcel, crimping the foil edges together in the center. Leave to stand for 30 minutes.

Place the foil parcels on the grid. Barbecue for 20–25 minutes, or until the flesh flakes easily when tested with a fork. Serve with rice. *Serves 4–6*

SALADS AND SAUCES

To transform the main barbecue items into an enjoyable meal, you do need delicious salads, as barbecue space is too limited to provide large quantities of hot vegetables. Besides, salads complement food cooked to sizzling perfection on the grill, especially in hot summer weather. Original dressings can do double duty as dips, plus there are lots of marinades in this section which can also be used as basting sauces.

Left: Barbecue Bean Salad (page 96). Right: Tuna Salad Royale (page 98)

At serving time, fork the All Bran mixture into the beans and garnish with the onion rings. Pour the dressing over and serve at once. *Serves 4–6*

RADICCHIO AND PINEAPPLE PASTA SALAD

2 cups pasta shapes, in
3 colors if possible
8 radicchio or red lettuce leaves
2-inch length green part of leek,
thinly sliced
2 stalks of celery, trimmed
3 canned pineapple slices, chopped
$\frac{2}{3}$ cup Nutrigrain (wholewheat and raisins)

Cook the pasta shapes in plenty of boiling salted water as directed until tender. Drain well. Tear the radicchio into pieces. Blanch the leek slices in boiling water for 1 minute then drain. Slice the celery.

Combine the pasta, pineapple, radicchio, leek and celery in a salad bowl. Stir in the Nutrigrain just before serving. *Serves 4–6*

DRESSED BEAN AND ONION SALAD

$\frac{1}{4}$ cup butter or margarine
1 clove of garlic, finely chopped
$\frac{2}{3}$ cup All Bran, crushed
$\frac{1}{4}$ teaspoon salt
1 (8-oz.) can red kidney beans, drained
1 (8-oz.) can black-eye beans
or garbanzo beans, drained
1 lb. fresh or frozen green beans, sliced and
cooked

For the dressing:

$\frac{1}{2}$ teaspoon salt
pinch of pepper
$\frac{1}{2}$ teaspoon dried basil
$\frac{1}{2}$ teaspoon mustard powder
4 tablespoons white wine vinegar
1 tablespoon clear honey
6 tablespoons oil

For the garnish:

onion rings

Melt the butter in a skillet and use to fry the garlic for 2 minutes. Stir in the All Bran and salt and fry briskly for 2 minutes more. Leave to cool.

Rinse the canned beans and drain well. Mix with the green beans in a salad bowl and chill.

To make the dressing, combine the salt, pepper, basil, mustard, vinegar and honey in a bowl. Gradually beat in the oil.

TUNA AND PEPPER RICE

scant $\frac{1}{2}$ cup brown rice
scant $\frac{1}{2}$ cup long grain white rice
1 (7-oz.) can tuna, drained
$\frac{2}{3}$ cup chopped sweet pepper (if possible red,
green and yellow)
$\frac{2}{3}$ cup canned corn kernels
1 tablespoon lemon juice
2 tablespoons butter
1 clove of garlic, finely chopped
$\frac{1}{2}$ teaspoon salt
$\frac{1}{3}$ cup All Bran, crushed

Cook the brown and white rice together in boiling salted water for about 12 minutes, or until tender. Drain and rinse in cold water. Drain again.

Flake the tuna and gently combine with the rice, pepper, corn and lemon juice in a bowl.

Melt the butter in a skillet, add the garlic and fry gently until soft. Stir in the salt and All Bran and cook for 2 minutes. Leave to cool.

Just before serving, sprinkle the All Bran mixture over the rice salad. *Serves 4–6*

Above: Tuna and Pepper Rice. Center: Radicchio and Pineapple Pasta Salad. Below: Dressed Bean and Onion Salad

93

PRAWNIE OR SHRIMP AND PASTA SALAD

Illustrated on page 86

2⅔ cups green pasta spirals
1 scallion, trimmed
1 sweet red pepper, deseeded
1 sweet green pepper, deseeded
8 oz. prawnies or shrimp, defrosted
pinch of ground nutmeg
3 tablespoons mayonnaise
5 tablespoons sour cream
salt and freshly ground black pepper

Cook the pasta as directed in plenty of boiling salted water until tender. Drain, refresh with cold water and drain again. Chop the scallion and pepper flesh.

Combine the pasta, prawnies or shrimp, onion and pepper in a bowl and sprinkle on the nutmeg.

Mix together the mayonnaise and sour cream and season with salt and pepper if necessary. Pour over the salad ingredients and toss well. Line a salad bowl with lettuce leaves and pile up the seafood mixture in the center. *Serves 4*

LETTUCE, ORANGE AND ALMOND SALAD

1 Romaine lettuce
1 bunch of watercress
3 small oranges
¼ cup slivered almonds

For the dressing:

1 tablespoon finely chopped shallot
or scallion
3 tablespoons orange juice
4 tablespoons olive or nut oil
pinch of granulated sugar
sea salt and freshly ground black pepper

Cut the lettuce crossways into 1-inch slices. Divide the watercress into sprigs. Place the lettuce and watercress in a salad bowl.

Carefully peel the oranges, removing all pith. Halve them then cut in slices, saving any juice for the dressing. Lay the orange slices on the green salad. Scatter the almonds over; toasted first if liked.

To make the dressing, put the shallot, fruit juice, oil and sugar in a small screw-topped jar and shake vigorously until blended. Season generously with salt and pepper to taste. At serving time, pour the dressing over the salad and toss the ingredients lightly. *Serves 4–6*

FENNEL AND ORANGE SALAD

3 oranges
1 bunch of scallions, trimmed
1 large head of Florence fennel
4 oz. Swiss cheese
1 lettuce

For the dressing:

4 tablespoons olive oil
1 tablespoon wine vinegar
½ teaspoon granulated sugar
1 teaspoon mild mustard
salt and freshly ground black pepper

For the garnish:

sweet red pepper strips

Peel the oranges and divide into segments, discarding all pith. Chop the onions. Slice the fennel. Cut the cheese into strips.

Arrange the lettuce leaves, fennel, orange segments, onion and cheese in a salad bowl. Garnish with red pepper strips.

To make the dressing, put the oil, vinegar, sugar and mustard in a small screw-topped jar and shake well until blended. Season with salt and pepper to taste and pour over the salad at serving time. *Serves 4*

Variation
CHINESE ORANGE SALAD Substitute 1 small head of Chinese leaves for the fennel and omit the lettuce and cheese. Chop 4 canned water chestnuts. Add to the salad with ⅔ cup chopped cooked chicken or turkey and ⅓ cup chopped canned bamboo shoot. Stir 1 tablespoon soy sauce into the dressing and taste before adding more seasoning.

Above: Lettuce, Orange and Almond Salad. Below: Fennel and Orange Salad

BARBECUE BEAN SALAD

Illustrated on page 90

1 small head chicory
2 (15.9-oz.) cans beans in barbecue sauce
1 large sweet red pepper, deseeded
4 scallions
8 oz. boneless smoked chicken
or cooked chicken
juice of 1 lime or small lemon
5 tablespoons olive oil
salt and freshly ground black pepper
few tortilla or potato chips

For the garnish:

thin wedges of lime

Separate the chicory into leaves and arrange in a shallow bowl. Drain the beans to remove some of the excess sauce. Spoon the beans on to the chicory. Finely chop the pepper flesh. Trim the scallions and split them in half lengthways. Divide the chicken into strips. Scatter the onion, pepper and chicken strips over the beans.

Mix together the lime juice and olive oil and season. Sprinkle this dressing evenly over the salad. Roughly crush the tortilla chips, scatter over the salad and serve garnished. *Serves 4–6*

Variation

BEAN AND SMOKED MACKEREL SALAD Use smoked mackerel fillets for the chicken. Remove the skin and cut the flesh into strips. Add 1 teaspoon creamed horseradish to the dressing.

BROWN RICE SALAD

Illustrated on page 47

generous $\frac{3}{4}$ cup brown rice
3 scallions, trimmed
1 cup canned corn kernels
$\frac{2}{3}$ cup chopped sweet red pepper
$\frac{2}{3}$ chopped sweet green pepper
$\frac{1}{3}$ cup seedless golden raisins
$\frac{1}{4}$ cup slivered almonds, lightly toasted
3 tablespoons bottled curry sauce

Cook the rice as directed in plenty of boiling salted water until tender. Drain well and leave to cool.

Chop the onions and mix with the corn, pepper, golden raisins and almonds. Fork into the cooked rice with the curry sauce. Transfer to a bowl and chill before serving. *Serves 4–6*

Variations

FRUITY RICE AND MUSTARD SALAD Substitute chopped eating apple and halved canned mandarin orange segments for the red and green pepper. Omit the onions if wished and fork in 1 tablespoon bottled mild mustard sauce instead of the curry sauce.

WALNUT RICE SALAD Substitute long grain white rice for the brown rice, use seedless raisins in place of the golden raisins and 1 cup walnut pieces instead of the almonds and onions. Fork in 3 tablespoons Italian dressing and omit the bottled sauce.

CAULIFLOWER SUMMER SALAD

1 large cauliflower
$\frac{2}{3}$ cup cooked green peas
1 large carrot, coarsely grated
$\frac{1}{2}$ cup mayonnaise

For serving:

lettuce or chicory leaves
orange slices

Divide the cauliflower into florets and blanch these in boiling salted water for 2 minutes. Drain well and leave to cool. Mix together the cauliflower florets, peas and carrot and stir in the mayonnaise. Chill for 1 hour.

Line a serving bowl with lettuce or chicory leaves, spoon the cauliflower salad into the center and garnish with orange slices. *Serves 4*

ITALIAN MUSHROOM SALAD Take $1\frac{1}{2}$ cups small button mushrooms and trim the stems level with the caps. Core and chop 2 small eating apples and pit 8 black olives. Combine the mushrooms, apple and olives and stir in 5 tablespoons bottled garlic mayonnaise. Leave to stand for 1 hour. Transfer to a platter and line the edge of the dish with cucumber slices.

Cauliflower Summer Salad, Italian Mushroom Salad

ORIENTAL PASTA SALAD

2 cups pasta shells or short-cut macaroni
2 medium-sized carrots
6-inch length cucumber
1 (8-oz.) can pineapple chunks, drained
3 cups beansprouts

For the dressing:

$\frac{1}{2}$ cup oil
3 tablespoons orange juice
3 tablespoons syrup from the can of pineapple
1 tablespoon soy sauce
pinch of ground ginger
salt and freshly ground black pepper

For the garnish:

4 scallions, trimmed

Cook the pasta shapes in plenty of boiling salted water as directed, until just tender. Meanwhile, make the dressing. Combine the dressing ingredients in a screw-topped jar and shake well. Season with salt and pepper to taste if wished.

Drain the pasta and while it is still hot, stir in the dressing. Leave to cool.

Cut the carrots into wafer thin slices with a potato peeler or grate coarsely. Cut the cucumber into thin diagonal slices. Add the carrot and cucumber slices, the pineapple chunks and beansprouts to the dressed pasta and toss lightly. Transfer to a serving platter.

To make the garnish, cut the scallions down to a length of 2 inches. Chop the green parts finely and sprinkle over the salad. Make several cuts in each onion with a sharp knife, from the stalk end towards the base, stopping about $\frac{1}{4}$ inch from the bottom of the bulb. Put the cut onions into a bowl of iced water and leave until they open and curl to resemble lilies. Drain and use to garnish the salad.
Serves 4–6

TUNA SALAD ROYALE

Illustrated on page 90

1 medium-sized head radicchio or red lettuce
1 Romaine lettuce heart
1 (7-oz.) can tuna
2 (8-oz.) cans curried beans
8 button mushrooms, thinly sliced
4 canned anchovy fillets
2 hard-cooked eggs, shelled
1 tablespoon snipped chives

For the dressing:

3 tablespoons lemon juice
4 tablespoons olive oil
salt and freshly ground black pepper

Arrange the radicchio leaves on a large flat salad platter. Cut the lettuce heart into quarters and arrange these on top, radiating out from the center. Drain the tuna and flake roughly. Spoon the beans on to the salad leaves in 4 sections and top with tuna. Scatter the mushroom slices over the salad and add the anchovy fillets.

Separate the whites and yolks of the eggs, chop the whites and press the yolks through a sieve. Pile

Left: Melon and Shrimp Salad. Right: Grapefruit and Avocado Cups

up the eggs in the center of the salad platter.

For the dressing, combine the lemon juice and olive oil and season generously. Sprinkle over the salad and finish with the chives. *Serves 4*

GRAPEFRUIT AND AVOCADO CUPS

1 large grapefruit
1 large ripe avocado
3 scallions, trimmed

For the dressing:

1 teaspoon finely chopped mint or pinch of dried mint
pinch of dried basil
pinch of sugar
1 tablespoon vinegar
4 tablespoons oil
salt and freshly ground black pepper

For serving:

radicchio or red lettuce leaves

Peel the grapefruit and divide into segments, discarding the pith. Roughly chop the flesh. Peel and pit the avocado and dice the flesh. Slice the scallions. Gently combine the grapefruit, avocado and onion.

To make the dressing, place the mint, basil and sugar in a small bowl and stir in the vinegar. Leave for a few minutes, then beat in the oil and season with salt and pepper to taste. Pour over the grapefruit mixture and leave to stand for 5 minutes.

Line a serving bowl or individual dishes with radicchio leaves and spoon the grapefruit salad into the center. *Serves 4*

CARROT AND RAISIN SALAD Place ⅔ cup seedless raisins in a small bowl and pour over 5 tablespoons orange juice, 3 tablespoons oil and 1 tablespoon sherry. Sprinkle on ½ teaspoon ground nutmeg and stir well. Leave to stand for about 4 hours, or until the raisins are plump, stirring occasionally. Coarsely grate 1 lb. carrots into a salad bowl and fork in the raisin mixture. Season with salt and pepper to taste before serving. *Serves 4*

MELON AND SHRIMP SALAD

1 cup shelled cooked shrimp
1 small honeydew melon
1 slice from a large onion
2-inch length cucumber
pinch of dried dill weed
¼ cup roast salted peanuts

For the dressing:

large pinch of ground ginger
1 tablespoon wine vinegar
¼ teaspoon mild mustard
pinch of sugar
⅔ cup light cream
salt and lemon pepper

For serving:

8 oz. shrimp in the shell
large sprig of parsley

Defrost the shellfish if necessary. Halve the melon, discard the seeds then remove the flesh and cut into dice. Divide the onion slice into rings and cut these into strips. Dice the cucumber. Place the melon, shrimp, onion and cucumber in a bowl.

For the dressing, stir the ginger, vinegar, mustard and sugar into the cream and season with salt and lemon pepper to taste. Pour over the melon mixture and toss lightly. Transfer to a serving dish and arrange the shrimp in the shell around the edge. Sprinkle the salad with the dill, scatter the peanuts over the top and serve garnished with the parsley. *Serves 4–6*

CURRY SAUCE

¼ cup butter
1 medium-sized onion, finely chopped
2 medium-sized carrots, coarsely grated
1 teaspoon curry powder
⅓ cup all-purpose flour
2 cups chicken bouillon
3 tablespoons tomato catsup
salt and freshly ground black pepper

Melt the butter in a pan and use to cook the onion and carrot gently until soft. Sprinkle in the curry powder and leave to cook over low heat for 3 minutes. Stir in the flour, then blend in the stock and catsup. Bring to a boil, stirring all the time. Season with salt and pepper to taste. This sauce can be kept warm in a foil container on the side of the barbecue. *Serves 4–6*

RED CURRANT SWEET AND SOUR SAUCE

2 tablespoons butter
1 medium-sized onion, very finely chopped
3 tablespoons malt vinegar
3 tablespoons spicy brown table sauce
½ cup sugar
½ teaspoon salt
4 tablespoons red currant jelly

Melt the butter in a pan and use to cook the onion gently until soft. Add the remaining ingredients and stir over low heat until the red currant jelly has melted. Cover and simmer for 30 minutes, or until the onion is reduced to a pulp and the sauce is smooth and slightly thickened. Transfer to a foil container and keep warm near the barbecue. *Serves 4–6*

MINT AND YOGURT MARINADE FOR LAMB

2 cloves of garlic, crushed
1 teaspoon lemon juice
1 tablespoon ready-to-use mint sauce
⅔ cup plain yogurt
salt and freshly ground black pepper (optional)

Mix the garlic, lemon juice and mint sauce into the yogurt. Season with salt and pepper to taste if wished. Pour over lamb in a shallow dish. Cover and leave to stand for about 8 hours, turning the meat occasionally. *Makes enough to marinate 1½ lb. boneless lamb in cubes or 12 lamb chops*

SPICED RED PLUM SAUCE

1 tablespoon oil
1 medium-sized onion, finely chopped
1 (15-oz.) can red plums in syrup
2 teaspoons soy sauce
pinch of ground ginger
pinch of ground cinnamon
salt and freshly ground black pepper (optional)

Heat the oil in a small pan and use to fry the onion gently until soft and just turning golden. Drain the plums, reserving the syrup. Press the fruit through a sieve to remove the pits. Add the fruit purée and syrup to the pan with soy sauce, ginger and cinnamon. Cook over low heat for 5 minutes, stirring frequently. Season with salt and pepper to taste if wished. *Serves 4–6*

PIMENTO YOGURT DRESSING

6-inch length of cucumber, peeled
2 canned red pimentos, sliced
1 tablespoon liquid from the pimento can
⅔ cup plain yogurt
salt and freshly ground black pepper

Roughly slice the cucumber then purée in a blender or food processor with the pimento, liquid from the can and the yogurt. Season with salt and pepper to taste.

CARIBBEAN CREAM DRESSING

1 teaspoon curry powder
3 tablespoons wine vinegar
1 teaspoon granulated sugar
3 tablespoons fresh lime juice
⅔ cup sour cream
4 scallions, trimmed
salt
1 slice of lime (optional)

Place the curry powder in a bowl and gradually mix in the vinegar, sugar, lime juice and sour cream. Chop the onions, stir most into the dressing and add salt to taste. Serve with the remaining onion sprinkled on top and float a slice of lime on the surface if wished.
Note: If fresh lime juice is not available, use lime juice cordial and omit the sugar.

TURKISH YOGURT DRESSING

12 black olives, pitted
12 canned anchovies
1 clove of garlic, finely chopped
⅔ cup plain yogurt
freshly ground black pepper

Finely chop the olives and anchovies and mix with the garlic. Stir in the yogurt and a grind or two of pepper to taste. Chill for 30 minutes to allow the flavors to blend before serving.

HERBY RED WINE MARINADE FOR BEEF

⅔ cup red wine
3 tablespoons red wine vinegar
3 tablespoons lemon juice
3 tablespoons oil
3 tablespoons chopped parsley
1 teaspoon dried mixed herbs
salt and freshly ground black pepper

Combine all the ingredients, except the seasoning, and leave to stand for 10 minutes. Season with salt and pepper to taste. Pour over beef in a shallow dish. Cover and leave to stand for at least 6 hours, turning the meat occasionally.

Caribbean Cream Dressing, Pimento Yogurt Dressing, Turkish Yogurt Dressing – all ideal with pasta salad

EXTRA DELIGHTS

To make a great success of your barbecue meal, there are many super items which you can prepare in your own kitchen beforehand. Home-made relishes, pickles and chutneys are particularly appropriate, and if the recipes are easy enough, it is well worth the trouble. Although potatoes baked in their skins are usually considered a "must", it is not easy to estimate the cooking time successfully, or find room for potato parcels in the ashes. Experience has shown that it is best to cook them, either in the conventional oven or microwave, and keep them hot in an insulated bag, with a "hot pack" if possible, until serving time. Then just slash open the tops and fill with one of my toppings or butters.

Among the other extra delights given here are some scrumptious sweets and desserts.

Above: Canned Corn Chutney (page 107). Below: Tomato and Cucumber Chutney (page 107)

STEAKS WITH APRICOT TOPPERS

½ (2½-oz.) pack savory butter with herbs and garlic
4 (4-oz.) sirloin steaks
8 canned apricot halves and 3 tablespoons apricot syrup from the can

Cut the block of savory butter into 8 pieces. Brush the steaks with the apricot syrup and arrange in a foil grill tray. Barbecue for about 4 minutes, then turn the steaks.

If necessary, cut a sliver from the rounded side of each apricot half so that it will stand firmly with the hollow upwards. Position 2 apricot 'cups' on each steak and put a piece of savory butter in each hollow. Barbecue for a further 4 minutes, or until the steak is done to your taste and the savory butter in the apricot cup begins to melt. Serve accompanied by MARINATED MUSHROOMS WITH HERB STUFFING. *Serves 4*

MARINATED MUSHROOMS WITH HERB STUFFING Take 6 large flat mushrooms, trim the stems level with the caps and chop the stem ends finely. Make up ½ cup parsley, thyme and lemon stuffing, mix with ⅓ cup hot water and leave to stand for 5 minutes. Combine with the chopped mushroom and 1 finely chopped stalk of celery. Stir together 4 tablespoons each oil and lemon juice and sprinkle this mixture all over the mushrooms. Leave to stand for at least 10 minutes. Fill the mushrooms with the celery stuffing and place on the grid. Barbecue for about 20 minutes, until the mushrooms soften and the filling is hot. At serving time, top each mushroom stem with a piece of savory butter with herbs and garlic and serve as it melts.

All-purpose barbecue butters

These are ideal for spreading between the partly cut slices of a French stick, which is then wrapped in foil and heated on the barbecue for about 20 minutes. Alternatively, place the butter on foil, form into rolls and chill. Slices are delicious, melting on barbecued meat or pressed into baked potatoes.

ORANGE AND OREGANO BUTTER

½ cup butter, softened
2 teaspoons finely chopped oregano or ½ teaspoon dried oregano
1 teaspoon finely grated orange rind
salt and freshly ground black pepper

Cream the butter in a bowl with the herb and orange rind. Season with salt and pepper to taste. Use immediately for hot barbecued bread, or turn out on a sheet of foil and form into a roll about 1½ inches in diameter. Chill until firm. Slice and serve on meat or potatoes. *Serves 4–6*

Variations
GARLIC AND HERB BUTTER Substitute 2 cloves of garlic for the orange rind. Chop very finely and beat into the butter with 2 teaspoons finely chopped mixed herbs or ½ teaspoon dried mixed herbs in place of oregano.

PAPRIKA AND PARSLEY BUTTER Substitute 1 teaspoon sweet paprika pepper for the orange rind and use 1 tablespoon very finely chopped parsley for the oregano. Season with garlic salt and pepper.

BARBECUED POTATO SLICES

1½ lb. potatoes, scrubbed
⅓ cup butter
4 tablespoons oil
1 teaspoon garlic salt

Cut the potatoes into ½-inch slices and place in a bowl. Melt the butter and stir in the oil and garlic salt. Pour over the potatoes and stir quickly until all the slices are coated.

Arrange the potato slices on the grid and barbecue for about 30 minutes, turning and brushing occasionally with the butter mixture left in the bowl, until brown and tender. *Serves 4–6*

Variation
PAPRIKA POTATO SLICES Substitute 1 teaspoon sweet paprika pepper for the garlic salt and add onion salt to taste.

Above right: Pastry Twists (page 108). Left: Marinated Mushrooms with Herb Stuffing. Below: Steaks with Apricot Toppers

COLORFUL GARDEN PICKLE

2¼ lb. prepared vegetables, such as red onion slices, broccoli, calabrese or cauliflower florets, carrot slices
salt
bay leaves
whole allspice berries or cloves
about 2½ cups pickling malt vinegar

Put the vegetables into a bowl and sprinkle liberally with salt. Leave to stand for 24–36 hours in a cool place.

Colorful Garden Pickle, Instant Pickled Beet Slices

Rinse the salty juices off the vegetables and drain really well. Arrange in jars to make a colorful selection and push a bay leaf and an allspice berry into each jar. Fill the jars with cold pickling vinegar, then seal and label.

Store for at least 2 weeks before using. *Makes about 3¼ lb.*

INSTANT PICKLED BEET SLICES Peel cooked beet, slice and pack into a jar. An empty pickling malt vinegar jar is ideal. Top up with cold pickling vinegar to cover the beet, then seal and leave for about 24 hours before using.

TOMATO AND CUCUMBER CHUTNEY

Illustrated on page 102

2¼ lb. red tomatoes, skinned
½ sweet red pepper, deseeded
⅓ cup salt
2½ cups water
scant 2 cups pickling malt vinegar
1 clove of garlic, crushed
1½ cups white sugar
½ teaspoon sweet paprika pepper
6-inch length of cucumber, sliced

Cut each tomato into 4 slices. Chop the pepper.

Stir the salt into the water until dissolved. Add the tomato slices and pepper flesh, then leave to stand for 2 hours. Drain and rinse off the salty liquid with cold water. Drain well.

Put the vinegar, garlic, sugar and paprika into a pan and heat gently, stirring, until the sugar has dissolved. Bring to a boil, add the tomato and pepper pieces, bring back to a boil and cook for 2 minutes. Put in the cucumber slices and cook for a further 1 minute. Lift out the tomato, pepper and cucumber mixture with a slotted spoon and transfer to warm clean jars.

Boil the vinegar liquid left in the pan until it begins to thicken, then strain over the tomato mixture to fill the jars. Seal, label and store for at least 1 week. Shake well before using. *Makes about 2¾ lb.*

CANNED CORN CHUTNEY

Illustrated on page 102

1 sweet green pepper, deseeded
1¼ cups pickling malt vinegar
1 teaspoon salt
½ cup white sugar
1 (11-oz.) can corn kernels, drained
1 canned red pimento, very finely chopped
1 teaspoon cornstarch
2 teaspoons water

Finely dice the pepper flesh. Put the vinegar, salt and sugar into a pan and heat gently, stirring until the sugar has dissolved. Bring to a fast boil, add the pepper, bring back to a boil and cook hard for 2 minutes, stirring constantly. Add the corn and pimento, bring back to a boil again and cook hard for 1 minute. Blend the cornstarch with the water, stir into the chutney and cook for a further 2 minutes, stirring all the time.

Transfer to jars, seal and label. This quick chutney can be used after 24 hours. *Makes about 1¼ lb.*

BAKED POTATO SKIN TOPPINGS

CREAM CHEESE AND PIMENTO Beat ¼ cup herbs and garlic savory butter with ½ cup cream cheese until fluffy. Drain and chop 1 canned red pimento and fork into the cheese mixture. Pile up in a small dish.

SEASONED SOUR CREAM AND CHIVES Stir 1¼ cups sour cream until smooth, then add 1 tablespoon lemon juice, a pinch of salt and 1 tablespoon granulated sugar. Stir in 3–4 tablespoons snipped chives or serve these in a separate small dish for sprinkling on the topped potatoes.

COTTAGE CHEESE AND MUSHROOM TOPPING Cream ¼ cup savory butter with black pepper until really soft. Beat in 1 cup sieved cottage cheese, ½ cup finely chopped mushrooms and 3 tablespoons grated onion. Season with extra salt and pepper if needed. Serve in a small dish.

SPICED CHEDDAR CHEESE TOPPING Beat ⅓ cup butter or margarine until soft. Beat 1½ cups finely grated sharp Cheddar cheese into the butter with ½ teaspoon ground allspice, ½ teaspoon dry mustard powder and 1 teaspoon clear honey. Pile up in a small dish and lift the surface into peaks with the tip of a knife. Sprinkle with a little paprika pepper before serving.

SAVORY BUTTERED PINEAPPLE TOPPING Drain 1 (13½-oz.) can of crushed pineapple really well. Melt ½ cup herbs and garlic savory butter until just soft enough to pour but not oily. Stir in the pineapple and heat through, stirring. Keep warm on the side of the barbecue in a small pan.

Quantities will very approximately serve 6–12

PASTRY TWISTS

Illustrated on page 105

1 cup all-purpose flour
2 tablespoons butter
2 tablespoons light brown sugar
5 tablespoons cold water

Sift the flour into a bowl and cut in the butter until the mixture resembles bread crumbs. Stir in the sugar, add the water and mix to a dough. Warm the jam and place in a small bowl.

Roll the dough out on a floured surface and cut into thin strips. Wind these closely round greased wooden sticks or peeled twigs. Place on the grid and barbecue for 4–6 minutes, turning once or twice during this time, until the pastry looks dry and is turning golden brown. Gently push the twists off the sticks and serve with warmed and sieved plum or raspberry jam dip. *Serves 4*

Variation
SAVORY TWISTS Substitute $\frac{1}{4}$ cup grated hard cheese for the sugar. Serve with a barbecue sauce or mild mustard sauce dip.

BRAN ROLLS

Illustrated on page 49

1 cake compressed yeast
1 teaspoon granulated sugar
scant 2 cups warm water
5 cups white or brown bread flour
2 teaspoons salt
2 tablespoons butter or margarine
$1\frac{1}{2}$ cups crushed bran flakes
1 egg, beaten
poppy seeds

Cream the yeast and sugar together to form a paste, then gradually mix in the water and stir until blended. Set aside in a warm place.

Place the flour and salt in a bowl and cut in the fat until the mixture resembles bread crumbs. Stir in the crushed flakes and yeast liquid and mix to a soft but manageable dough. Turn out on a floured surface and knead for 10 minutes. Place the dough in a bowl, cover loosely with a large plastic bag and leave in a warm place until double in size.

Turn out on a lightly floured surface and knead

gently for 3–4 minutes. Divide into 7 equal portions and shape each into a 4-inch square. Cut the squares in half diagonally to make triangles. Alternatively, divide the dough into 14 equal-sized portions and shape each into a ball.

Arrange the rolls on greased cookie sheets and leave in a warm place for about 30 minutes, until puffy. Brush with egg and sprinkle with poppy seeds.

Bake in a preheated hot oven (450°F) for about 12 minutes, or until golden brown. If they are ready, the rolls will sound hollow when tapped on the base with your knuckles. Cool on a wire rack. Ideal to serve with triangular HARVEST BURGERS (see page 48). *Makes about 14*

APRICOT AND NUT STUFFED FRUIT BREAD

1 cup dried apricots
$\frac{2}{3}$ cup chopped preserved ginger
$\frac{1}{4}$ cup unsalted butter
$\frac{1}{4}$ cup slivered almonds
2 fruited loaves

Place the apricots, ginger and butter in a blender or food processor and switch on until the mixture is almost smooth. Stir in the almonds.

Slice the loaves at $\frac{3}{4}$-inch intervals, cutting about three-quarters of the way through each time. Spread the apricot mixture between the slices of bread.

Wrap the loaves individually in aluminum foil with the shiny side inwards. Seal to make airtight parcels and place on the grid. Barbecue for about 20 minutes, turning the parcels over occasionally. Unwrap and serve slices with fruit salad. *Serves 8–10*

BARBECUED CORN IN THE HUSK Allow 1 corn cob and 2 tablespoons butter per person. Pull back the husk leaves of each cob and remove the silky threads. Spread the kernels with softened butter, season with salt and pepper and refold the husk leaves over the corn on the cob. Thread each cob on a separate skewer, securing the leaves by pushing the skewer through them at the rounded end. Roast over the barbecue for about 40 minutes, turning frequently, until the husks char. Strip off the husks and continue cooking the corn on the cob for a further 5–10 minutes, or until the kernels are just golden. Serve on the skewers.

Apricot and Nut Stuffed Fruit Bread

BARBECUED FRUIT SALAD

Illustrated on page 84

selection of prepared fresh fruit such as red cherries, diced eating apple, orange segments, halved strawberries, halved and pitted grapes, total prepared weight 1½ lb. (4 cups)
⅓ cup granulated sugar
3 tablespoons lemon juice
⅔ cup water
3 tablespoons sweet sherry

For the topping:

5 tablespoons light brown sugar

Divide the fruit mixture between 2 shaped foil trays. Put the white sugar in a pan with the lemon juice and water. Heat gently, stirring, until the sugar has dissolved. Boil for 4 minutes then remove from the heat and stir in the sherry. Spoon the syrup over the trays of fruit and leave to cool.

When required, set the trays on the grid and sprinkle with the brown sugar. Barbecue for about 15 minutes, or until piping hot. *Serves 4–6*

SUMMER ORANGE AND ROSE SALAD

4 large oranges
1¼ cups water
½ cup granulated sugar
1 tablespoon lemon juice
5 tablespoons orange liqueur
1 tablespoon triple-distilled rose water

Pare the rind of the oranges and cut into very thin strips. Boil these in a pan of water for 10 minutes. Drain, refresh in cold water and drain again.

Peel the oranges and divide into segments, discarding all pith and pips. Place the segments in a serving dish.

Put the water in a pan and stir in the sugar and lemon juice. Heat gently, stirring, until the sugar has dissolved. Add the strips of rind and boil until the syrup is sufficiently reduced to coat the back of a spoon. Stir in the liqueur, remove from the heat and add the rose water. Spoon the syrup over the orange segments. Chill. *Serves 4–6*

BUTTERSCOTCH DIP

⅓ cup butter
¾ cup light brown sugar
¾ cup unsweetened evaporated milk

For serving:

wedges of eating apple
slices of banana
marshmallows
ladyfingers

Put the butter in a small pan and heat gently until melted. Add the sugar and half the milk and stir over low heat until the sugar has dissolved. Blend in the remaining milk. Keep warm on the side of the barbecue.

Spear pieces of fruit or marshmallows on long-handled forks, or hold ladyfingers, and dip into the butterscotch mixture. *Serves 4–6*

Variation
RICH CHOCOLATE DIP Make the butterscotch dip as above. Add ⅔–1 cup semi-sweet chocolate pieces to the butterscotch dip while it is still fairly hot. Stir gently until the chocolate melts and the dip is smooth again. Transfer to a warm serving dish and keep hot. Serve as above.

Butterscotch Dip

110

BARBECUE MENUS FOR GUESTS

The invitation – come to a party – is so easy to issue when you've a barbecue in mind. The food is such fun to prepare and there is no need for you or your guests to dress up, since informality is the keynote of al fresco entertaining.

Halloween Barbecue (page 114)

HALLOWEEN BARBECUE

Illustrated on page 112

Whether you use a scooped-out pumpkin as a lantern or as a fun container for soup, be sure to take apples along to the barbecue and keep the children happy while the food is sizzling by letting them play the old apple-bobbing game.

TURKEY KEBABS WITH BEER BASTE

1½ lb. turkey breast roll
2 cups dark beer
1 large onion, finely chopped
⅓ cup oil
2 teaspoons hot mustard
6 zucchini
12 cherry tomatoes
1 tablespoon cornstarch
salt and freshly ground black pepper
little extra oil

Defrost the turkey roast if necessary. Discard the plastic casing and cut the meat into large chunks. Place in a shallow dish. Mix together the beer, onion, oil and mustard. Pour over the turkey pieces, cover and leave to stand for about 2 hours.

Top and tail the zucchini and cut into 1-inch pieces. Lift out the turkey chunks and thread on skewers, alternating with pieces of zucchini and tomatoes. Brush all the ingredients generously with marinade.

Moisten the cornstarch with a little water. Place the remaining marinade in a pan and boil for 3 minutes. Add the blended cornstarch and stir until thickened. Season with salt and pepper to taste. Keep warm near the barbecue.

Arrange the kebabs on the greased grid. Barbecue for about 20 minutes, turning frequently and brushing with a little oil if necessary, until the turkey is cooked through. Serve with the sauce. *Serves 6*

TOASTED MARSHMALLOWS Spear marshmallows on long forks and hold over the barbecue until melting slightly. Allow to cool until deliciously gooey, then dip into bowls of chopped nuts or toasted coconut shreds. Take care to cool the melting marshmallows before eating.

CIDER AND TURKEY SOUP

1 turkey carcass or a turkey soup pack (neck, giblets, heart, etc.)
5 cups water
2 large onions, sliced
2 carrots, chopped
1 bay leaf
3 tablespoons butter or margarine
⅓ cup all-purpose flour
⅔ cup hard cider
¼ teaspoon ground mace
celery salt and freshly ground black pepper
½ cup finely chopped cooked turkey
⅔ cup light cream
sweet paprika pepper for sprinkling

Defrost the turkey soup pack if necessary. Place the carcass or soup pack in a large pan with the water, half the onion and carrot and the bay leaf. Bring to a boil, skim the surface, cover and simmer for about 1 hour. Strain off and reserve 3¾ cups of the stock.

Melt the butter in a separate pan and use to fry the remaining onion and carrot gently for 3 minutes. Sprinkle in the flour, stir well and cook for 1 minute. Gradually add the stock and cider and bring to a boil, stirring constantly. Season well with the mace, celery salt and pepper to taste, then cover and simmer for 20 minutes.

Sieve or blend the soup and return it to the pan with the turkey meat. Bring to boiling point, stir in the cream and adjust the seasoning if necessary. Simmer for 2 minutes, then keep hot in the covered pan near the barbecue. Sprinkle portions of soup lightly with paprika. *Serves 4–6*

RIBBONED TURKEY SAUSAGES WITH DIPS

1 (14-oz.) pack uncooked pastry dough
12 turkey links
1 egg, beaten

Defrost the pastry if necessary, then roll out thinly and cut into ½-inch wide strips. Wrap strips of pastry around the sausages and place on a cookie sheet. Brush with beaten egg. Bake in a preheated moderately hot oven (400°F) for about 35 minutes, or until well browned. Serve warm or cold with

SPICED CRANBERRY, CORN AND PEPPER and CURRY CHEESE DIPS (see below). *Serves 4–6*

SPICED CRANBERRY DIP Mash 1 (6½-oz.) jar of jellied cranberry sauce with ¼ teaspoon ground mace then transfer to a small dish.

CORN AND PEPPER DIP Mix together ⅓ cup cream cheese and 3 tablespoons mayonnaise. Stir in 1 tablespoon finely chopped sweet red pepper and 4 tablespoons canned corn kernels. Season with salt and pepper to taste and place in a small dish.

CURRY CHEESE DIP Mix together 1 teaspoon concentrated curry sauce and 1 cup cottage cheese. Chop 1 tablespoon mango chutney, stir into the cheese mixture and transfer to a small dish.

BIRTHDAY BARBECUE

It's so easy to create a birthday party menu using broiled and skewered food taken from our large selection. Have lots of sliced fresh bread, a big green salad and cobs of corn with a basting sauce.

The picture above shows you easy dress-ups to give the meal more of a party feel.

STUFFED CHEESE BALL Remove the top of a small Edam cheese and carefully scoop out the center.

Birthday Barbecue

Vandyke the edge with a small sharp knife. Dice the cheese you have removed and set aside the neat dice. Place the remainder in a blender or food processor with an equal quantity of mayonnaise. Blend until smooth. Use to fill the cheese ball and top with black olives. Place on a serving dish and surround with vegetable crudités as dippers.

PEPPERY PINEAPPLE TOSS Combine half the cheese dice with 1 small sweet red pepper, deseeded and cut into diamond-shaped pieces. Cook 1⅓ cups pasta spirals in plenty of boiling salted water. Drain, refresh with cold water and drain again. Mix together the pasta, cheese and pepper and fold in ½ cup canned pineapple pieces. Stir 3 tablespoons Italian dressing into an equal quantity of pineapple syrup. Pour over the pasta salad and toss the ingredients lightly.

CHEESE AND VEGETABLE RING Arrange a bed of shredded lettuce on a round serving plate. Combine finely sliced raw zucchini, mushroom and tomato and pile up on the lettuce. Surround with a ring of cheese dice. This makes a fresh crunchy addition to barbecued pork chops or kebabs.

To make a fine finish, load skewers with unpeeled wedges of nectarine and brush with melted peach jam. Place on a foil lined grill pan and barbecue until the fruit is hot.

BONFIRE BARBECUE

Just as good for other special occasions where the children are all-important. This selection of recipes will really hit the spot as far as they are concerned.

GOULASH SOUP

1 lb. ground beef
1 large onion, chopped
1 clove of garlic, crushed
3 tablespoons flour
1 tablespoon sweet paprika pepper
$\frac{1}{4}$ teaspoon dried marjoram
$\frac{1}{2}$ teaspoon caraway seeds (optional)
1 (14-oz.) can tomatoes
$3\frac{3}{4}$ cups beef bouillon
1 sweet green pepper, deseeded
1 lb. potatoes, peeled and diced
1 teaspoon tomato paste
salt and freshly ground black pepper

For serving:

$\frac{2}{3}$ cup sour cream

Put the beef into a large pan and cook over low heat, stirring frequently, until it looks brown and crumbly. If necessary spoon off excess fat. Add the onion and garlic to the meat and cook for 3 minutes, stirring occasionally. Sprinkle in the flour, paprika, marjoram and caraway seeds and stir well over the heat for 1 minute. Add the tomatoes and liquid from the can and the stock. Bring to a boil, stirring, cover and simmer for 30 minutes.

Chop the pepper flesh and add to the soup with the potatoes and tomato paste. Stir well, bring back to boiling point, cover and continue cooking for a further 20 minutes, or until the potato is tender. Taste and season with salt and pepper. Keep warm near the barbecue. Serve in mugs or bowls and top with sour cream. *Serves 6–8*

HAM AND CHEESE STUFFED POTATOES Mix together $\frac{1}{3}$ cup finely chopped ham, $\frac{1}{4}$ cup butter and 1 cup finely grated Cheddar cheese. Place on a sheet of foil, form into a flat layer and chill until firm. Bake 6 large potatoes until tender. Cut a deep cross in the top of each potato and squeeze from the sides to open the cuts. Stamp out fancy shapes from the ham butter using cocktail cutters and press these into the potato. *Serves 6*

LAMB CHOPS WITH MINTED ONION SAUCE

1 ($\frac{3}{4}$-oz.) pack onion sauce mix
$1\frac{1}{4}$ cups milk
1 medium-sized onion, finely chopped
1 tablespoon sweet mint jelly
salt and freshly ground black pepper
chopped parsley
6 large loin of lamb chops
tomato wedges

Place the sauce mix in a pan and gradually blend in the milk. Bring to a boil, stirring. Mix in the onion, cover and simmer for about 10 minutes, or until the onion is tender. Blend in the mint jelly and season with salt and pepper if necessary. Place in a small pan, sprinkle with parsley and keep warm on the side of the barbecue.

Arrange the chops on the greased grid. Barbecue for about 20 minutes, turning them once, or until cooked to taste. Transfer to a platter, garnish with tomato wedges and serve with the sauce. *Serves 6*

CHEESE AND TUNA PASTA SALAD

2 cups pasta bows or shells
1 (7-oz.) can tuna, drained
6 oz. sharp Cheddar cheese, cubed
1 medium-sized onion, grated
6-inch length cucumber, diced
3 tablespoons mayonnaise
$\frac{2}{3}$ cup plain yogurt
few drops of Worcestershire sauce

For serving:

lettuce leaves
cucumber slices
parsley or snipped chives

Cook the pasta as directed in plenty of boiling salted water until tender. Drain, refresh with cold water and drain again. Leave to cool.

Flake the tuna and fold into the pasta with the cheese, onion and cucumber. Combine the mayonnaise, yogurt and Worcestershire sauce and fold into the pasta mixture.

Line a serving dish with lettuce leaves and cucumber slices, pile up the salad in the center and sprinkle with the parsley or chives. *Serves 6*

Bonfire Barbecue

IMPROMPTU STORECUPBOARD BARBECUE

When you make a sudden decision to set up the barbecue and there is no time for a special shopping expedition, most of the ingredients can come from your storage shelves or freezer. These recipes suggest new and delicious ways to use canned meat and soups to stretch the menu.

MIXED BARBECUE MEATS WITH THREE DIPS

Barbecue a selection of small meat cuts, such as 4-oz. rump steak portions, breaded turkey escalopes or chicken drumsticks, chicken and mushroom kebabs. See chart on page 34 for cooking times. Serve with three tasty barbecue dips.

CURRIED CHICKEN DIP Core and grate 1 eating apple and mix with 2 teaspoons lemon juice.

Gradually stir in 1 (5½-oz.) can condensed cream of chicken soup (undiluted), 1 tablespoon chopped mango chutney and 2 teaspoons concentrated curry sauce. Mix well, transfer to a serving bowl and sprinkle with a little chopped parsley or mint.

CHILI AND HAM DIP Place 1 (10-oz.) can concentrated tomato soup in a blender or food processor with ⅓ cup diced cooked ham, 1 teaspoon chili sauce and 1 teaspoon granulated sugar. Process until smooth and transfer to a serving bowl. If liked, top with canned mushroom slices or chopped scallions.

TANGY AVOCADO DIP Deseed and chop the flesh of ½ small sweet green pepper and 3 scallions. Halve and pit 1 large or 2 small avocados, reserving the avocado shells. Place the avocado, pepper and onion in a blender or food processor with 1 (10-oz.) can condensed cream of celery soup, ½ teaspoon Worcestershire sauce, 1 teaspoon wine

Impromptu Storecupboard Barbecue

vinegar and 1 tablespoon lemon juice. Blend until smooth and season with salt and pepper if desired. Fill the avocado shells with the dip and sprinkle a little sweet paprika on the surface. This dip is best if prepared only 1 hour before serving time.

QUICK FRENCH BREAD PIZZAS

1 small crusty French stick (12 inches long)
1 (8-oz.) can tomatoes, drained
3 tablespoons tomato paste
$\frac{1}{2}$ teaspoon sugar
1 cup diced cooked ham
1 ($7\frac{1}{2}$-oz.) can small button mushrooms in brine, drained
salt and freshly ground black pepper
4 oz. Mozzarella cheese, sliced

Cut the stick in half crossways, then split each half lengthways to give 4 quarters. Trim off the rounded end from each piece.

Roughly chop the tomatoes and mix with the tomato paste and sugar. Spread on the bread bases. Combine the ham dice and mushrooms and divide evenly among the pizzas. Season with salt and pepper to taste, then top with the cheese slices. Place under a hot broiler until the cheese melts.

Arrange a bed of lettuce leaves on a platter, top with the pizzas and garnish with tomato wedges. Delicious hot or cold. *Serves 4*

CHEESE AND BEEF PATTIES

1 (15-oz.) can ground beef in gravy
1 medium-sized onion, finely chopped
$1\frac{1}{2}$ cups fresh bread crumbs
$\frac{3}{4}$ cup grated Cheddar cheese
salt and freshly ground black pepper
little flour
oil

For the sauce:

1 (10-oz.) can mushroom soup
3 tablespoons sour cream
few drops of Worcestershire sauce

Put the beef in gravy into a pan and heat gently, stirring, until almost boiling. Leave to cool.

Put the onion, bread crumbs and cheese in a bowl and gradually mix in the meat and gravy. When well combined, season with salt and pepper.

Divide the mixture into 6 equal portions and shape each into a round flat cake on a floured surface. Coat all over in flour and transfer to a cookie sheet lined with foil. Cover and chill thoroughly for at least 1 hour.

Meanwhile, bring the soup to boiling point in a pan, remove from the heat and stir in the cream and Worcestershire sauce. Transfer to a serving dish.

Brush the patties with oil and arrange on a greased grid. Barbecue for about 15 minutes, turning carefully half-way through cooking time. Serve with the tangy sauce. *Serves 4–6*

CHILLED CHOCOLATE FUDGE CAKE

$2\frac{2}{3}$ cups semi-sweet chocolate pieces
1 lb. graham crackers, roughly crushed
$\frac{1}{3}$ cup granulated sugar
10 candied cherries, chopped
$\frac{1}{2}$ cup chopped walnuts
1 teaspoon instant coffee
1 ($7\frac{1}{2}$-oz.) can unsweetened evaporated milk
$\frac{1}{4}$ cup butter
2 eggs, beaten

For serving:

whipped cream
candied cherry pieces
2 walnut halves

Line a loaf-shaped pan measuring about 9 inches by 5 inches with foil.

Place the chocolate in a bowl over a pan of hot water until melted. Put the cracker crumbs, sugar, cherries, walnuts and coffee powder in a bowl. Pour the milk into a pan, add the butter and heat until the butter melts. Remove from the heat and gradually blend into the melted chocolate. Briskly stir in the egg. Pour over the dry ingredients in the bowl and mix well. Transfer to the prepared pan and press flat. Cover and chill for at least 8 hours.

Turn the cake out on a serving dish and strip off the foil. Decorate with piped rosettes of cream and top these with pieces of cherry and walnut. Serve cut into slices. *Serves 6–8*

SOUTH SEAS BARBECUE

Something just a little different from the very popular Chinese dishes many people enjoy, either in a restaurant or as a take-home meal.

LETTUCE TREASURES

8 large crisp lettuce leaves

For the filling:

1 sweet green pepper, deseeded
3 tablespoons oil
3 pieces preserved ginger, finely chopped
1 (6-oz.) can beansprouts, drained
1 teaspoon salt
pinch of sugar

For the filling, cut the pepper flesh into shreds. Heat the oil in a wok or large skillet until very hot and use to fry the ginger and pepper for about 15 seconds. Add the beansprouts, salt and sugar and stir-fry for 1 minute. Remove from the heat.

Divide the filling among the lettuce leaves and roll each one up, folding in the edges, to make neat parcels. Serve warm or cold.

MALAYAN CURRIED CHICKEN

1 (3–3½-lb.) chicken
5 tablespoons oil
1 large onion, thinly sliced
2 cloves of garlic, crushed
3 tablespoons Chinese curry powder
1¼ cups chicken bouillon
1 sweet red pepper, deseeded
1 tablespoon cornstarch
3 tablespoons soy sauce
pinch of sugar
1 (8-oz.) can pineapple chunks
4 tablespoons creamed coconut

Using poultry shears, divide the chicken into about 20 pieces.

Heat the oil in a large pan and use to stir-fry the onion and garlic for 1 minute. Remove the onion and garlic from the pan with a slotted spoon and reserve. Add the chicken pieces to the oil remaining in the pan and fry for about 2 minutes, turning the pieces frequently. Sprinkle in the curry powder and stir-fry for a further 1 minute. Pour in the stock and bring to a boil, stirring. Simmer for 15 minutes.

Cut the pepper flesh into strips. Blend the cornstarch with the soy sauce and add to the pan with the pepper strips, sugar, pineapple cubes, coconut cream and reserved onion and garlic. Stir until the curry returns to boiling point. Simmer for a further 5 minutes. Keep warm near the barbecue. Serve with rice. *Serves 4–6*

THREE HARMONY SATAY

8 oz. rump steak
8 oz. boneless lean lamb
8 oz. boneless lean pork
oil

For the dip:

⅔ cup peanut butter
1 tablespoon sesame oil
3 tablespoons chili sauce
3 tablespoons yellow bean sauce
3 tablespoons soy sauce
1 tablespoon sugar
1 tablespoon dry sherry

For serving:

sliced radishes
carrot sticks
cucumber sticks
assorted nuts
cooked long-grain rice

Cut the meat into small neat cubes. Have ready a bundle of 20–25 satay sticks or small peeled twigs and grease these lightly. Thread 5 to 6 cubes of meat on each and brush with oil.

Mix together all the ingredients for the dip and divide among small containers or shells. Arrange the vegetable and nut accompaniments in small dishes.

Place the loaded sticks on the grid. Barbecue, allowing 5–6 minutes for beef and 7–8 minutes for lamb and pork, and turning the sticks every 2 minutes, until done to taste. Arrange the cooked meat skewers on a bed of rice and serve with the side dishes and dip. *Serves 6*

South Seas Barbecue

CELESTIAL PINEAPPLE Cut 1 ripe pineapple in half lengthways, scoop out the flesh and cut into bite-sized pieces, discarding any woody core. Drain 1 (11-oz.) can of lychees. Remove the seeds from half a small watermelon and cut out the flesh with a melonballer. Mix together the syrup from the lychees and 3 tablespoons dark rum. Place the pineapple pieces, melon balls and lychees in a bowl and pour the rum syrup over. Leave to stand for about 20 minutes, then spoon the mixed fruit into the pineapple halves and serve on a tray lined with leaves. *Serves 6–8*

Accompany this barbecue with refreshing fruit drinks or exotic cocktails.

121

Duckling Barbecue

DUCKLING BARBECUE

Depending on the number of guests you invite, you may decide to opt for spit-roasting at least two ducklings plus some portions, or providing all portions. Delicious alternatives are the recipe given on page 85 for SPIT-ROAST DUCKLINGS WITH APRICOT GLAZE or the one given below for portions only.

SPICED ORANGE DUCKLING PORTIONS

4 duckling portions

For the sauce:

3 tablespoons light brown sugar
5 tablespoons soy sauce
$\frac{2}{3}$ cup orange juice
$\frac{2}{3}$ cup dry white wine
5 tablespoons water
$\frac{1}{2}$ teaspoon dry mustard powder
$\frac{1}{2}$ teaspoon sweet paprika pepper
$\frac{1}{4}$ teaspoon ground cinnamon
3–4 drops hot pepper sauce

Defrost the duckling portions if necessary. Mix together all the ingredients for the sauce and leave to stand for 1 hour.

Place the duck portions in a large plastic bag, add half the sauce, seal the bag securely and lay it in a shallow dish. Leave in a cool place for 2 hours, turning the bag over once during this time.

Snip a corner off the bag and drain excess marinade into a small dish. Use this for basting the duck during cooking. Arrange the duckling portions on the greased grid. Barbecue for about 50 minutes, brushing with the marinade and turning frequently, until cooked through.

Meanwhile, place the reserved half of the sauce in a pan and bring to simmering point, stirring frequently. Serve in a small jug. *Serves 4*

HERBY STUFFED TOMATOES

4 "steak" tomatoes, halved
$\frac{1}{2}$ cup parsley, thyme and lemon stuffing mix
$\frac{1}{3}$ cup hot water
1 stalk of celery, finely chopped
3 tablespoons chopped canned pineapple
little oil

Scoop the seeds from the tomato halves and discard. Combine the stuffing mix and hot water and leave to stand for 5 minutes. Combine with the celery and pineapple and use to fill the tomato halves. Sprinkle with a little oil. Place the stuffed tomato halves on the greased grid. Barbecue for about 20 minutes, until the tomatoes soften and the filling is hot.

GREEN AND WHITE DRESSED SALAD Cook generous 1 cup long grain white rice in plenty of boiling salted water until tender. Drain well. While the rice is cooking, make up $\frac{2}{3}$ cup Italian dressing. Pour over the rice while it is still warm, then leave to cool in a bowl. Cook 1 cup frozen peas in lightly salted water, drain and fold into the rice.

BANANAS WITH SYRUP AND GINGER

$\frac{1}{2}$ cup granulated sugar plus $\frac{1}{4}$ cup light brown sugar
4 tablespoons lemon juice
4 tablespoons water
$\frac{3}{4}$ cup roughly chopped preserved ginger
4 large bananas, sliced

Put the sugar in a pan and heat gently until melted. Add the lemon juice and water but take care as the mixture will bubble fiercely. Stir over low heat until the caramel has dissolved and the mixture is smooth. Add the ginger pieces.

Divide the banana slices among 4 large or 8 smaller heatproof dishes and spoon the ginger and syrup over them. Place the dishes near the barbecue if wished so that they become slightly warm. *Serves 4 or 8*

Variations
GINGERED ORANGES Substitute 4 large oranges for the bananas. Peel, then divide into segments, discarding any pith. Use orange juice in place of both the lemon juice and water to make the syrup. Serve sprinkled with slivered almonds.

SYRUPY PINEAPPLE WITH COCONUT Peel a large ripe pineapple, then slice and cut into chunks, discarding any woody core. Make the syrup as in the main recipe but omit the ginger. Spread 1 cup shredded coconut on a sheet of foil in a broiler pan and toast until golden. Leave to cool and sprinkle generously over the pineapple.

INDIAN STYLE BARBECUE

There's nothing tastier than the Indian dishes, redolent of spices, which make up this menu. It is ideal for an occasion when you prefer to make up and cook the dishes in advance in the oven, to reheat on the barbecue later.

BAKED INDIAN KEBABS

1 cup grated onion
2-inch length fresh root ginger, peeled
1 cup finely ground lamb or beef
pinch of sugar
½ teaspoon salt
1 tablespoon curry powder
2 cloves of garlic, very finely chopped
1 teaspoon ground turmeric
oil

For the dip:

⅔ cup plain yogurt
2 teaspoon chopped mint (from a jar) or
3 tablespoons finely chopped mint
salt
pinch of sugar
ground cumin or sweet paprika pepper for sprinkling

Put the grated onion into a cloth and squeeze out excess liquid. Grate the piece of ginger. Place the onion and ginger in a bowl with the meat, sugar, salt, curry powder, garlic and turmeric. Mix to combine, then knead the mixture for 2 minutes.

Line a cookie sheet with foil and brush this lightly with oil. Divide the meat mixture into 12 equal portions and form each into a sausage shape. Arrange well apart on the foil. Place the "sausages" in the oven with the Tandoori chicken when you reduce the temperature to moderate (350°F) and cook for 10 minutes. Turn and cook for a further 10 minutes. Like the Tandoori chicken pieces, these can be chilled for up to 4 hours and reheated on the barbecue for about 5 minutes.

For the dip, mix the yogurt and mint with a little salt to taste and the sugar in a glass ramekin dish and place in the center of a serving plate. Sprinkle the surface of the dip with ground cumin or paprika. Arrange the hot "kebabs" round the dip. *Serves 4*

MIXED VEGETABLE PILAFF

⅔ cup Basmati or long grain rice
1½ cups water
1 tablespoon oil
½-inch length cinnamon stick
2 whole cloves
½ teaspoon ground cardamom
6 cashew nuts, halved
6 whole almonds (not blanched)
1 tablespoon seedless golden raisins
½ cup frozen mixed vegetables, defrosted
salt

Wash the rice 5 times until the water is clear. Drain well. Place in a heatproof glass casserole, add the water and boil for 5 minutes. Reduce the heat, cover and simmer for 10 minutes.

Heat the oil in a skillet and use to fry the cinnamon stick, cloves and cardamom for 1 minute. Put in the cashews, almonds and golden raisins, stir over the heat for a few seconds then add the mixed vegetables. Sprinkle in a little salt to taste and cook gently for 5 minutes.

Lightly fork the spice mixture into the cooked rice, cover and keep warm. If necessary reheat on the side of the barbecue, or in a cool oven, in the heatproof glass casserole. *Serves 4*

TANDOORI CHICKEN

4 chicken portions, skinned

For the marinade:

1¼ cups plain yogurt
3 tablespoons tomato paste
2 teaspoons sweet paprika pepper
1 teaspoon mild chili powder
1 tablespoon lemon juice
1 teaspoon finely grated lemon rind
1 tablespoon orange juice
1 tablespoon finely grated orange rind
1 teaspoon salt
1 tablespoon grated fresh root ginger
1 teaspoon coarsely ground black pepper
2 cloves of garlic, finely chopped
few drops of red food coloring (optional)

Mix together all the ingredients for the marinade. Put the chicken portions in a glass bowl, pour the

Indian Style Barbecue

marinade over and turn until the chicken is completely coated. Cover and leave to stand for at least 8 hours.

Lay the chicken pieces in an ovenproof glass dish. Place in a preheated moderately hot oven (400°F). After 5 minutes, reduce the oven temperature to moderate (350°F) and bake for a further 10 minutes. Turn the chicken pieces and cook on for a further 10 minutes. Keep warm on the side of the barbecue or, if required for serving later, leave to cool. The chicken pieces can be kept in the refrigerator for up to 4 hours before reheating on

the barbecue for about 10 minutes, turning frequently. The yogurt and mint dip makes a good accompaniment to this dish also. *Serves 4*

INDIAN SIDE SALAD Arrange the following ingredients together in a bowl; lettuce leaves, tomato wedges, radish slices, chopped raw onion and garlic. Garnish with celery leaves and fresh coriander. Serve this "undressed" salad with the Tandoori chicken portions.

125

BIG CHICKEN BARBECUE

Just the job when a group of friends get together, each bringing one prepared dish for the feast. Divide the work between you and multiply the choices on the menu. A point to remember – someone needs to be responsible for the rice, bread and accompanying salads!

HERBED CHICKEN

scant 1 cup olive or corn oil
3 tablespoons lemon juice
1 teaspoon mild chili powder
2 cloves of garlic, crushed
generous pinch of dried rosemary, oregano,
tarragon and parsley
salt and freshly ground black pepper
4 chicken portions

Combine the oil, lemon juice, chili powder, garlic and herbs. Season with salt and pepper to taste. Score the chicken flesh with a sharp knife and place in a shallow dish. Coat with the herb mixture and leave to stand for at least 4 hours, turning twice during this time.

Drain off and reserve the marinade. Arrange the chicken portions on the grid. Barbecue for about 50 minutes, turning and brushing with the reserved marinade during cooking, until the juices run clear when tested. Serve with hot bread and an avocado dip. *Serves 4*

CHICKEN TIKKA WITH MINT AND CINNAMON SAUCE

4 boneless chicken breasts, skinned
5 tablespoons oil
2 large onions, sliced

For the marinade:

5 tablespoons curry paste
5 tablespoons plain yogurt

For the sauce:

$\frac{1}{4}$ teaspoon ground cinnamon
2 teaspoons concentrated mint sauce from a jar
$\frac{2}{3}$ cup plain yogurt

Cut each chicken breast in half horizontally to give 2 thick slices and place these in a shallow dish. Stir the curry paste into the yogurt until well blended, then pour over the chicken slices and stir until completely coated. Cover and leave for 24 hours.

For the sauce, stir the cinnamon into the mint sauce in a small bowl. When completely blended, gradually stir in the yogurt.

Heat the oil in a skillet and use to cook the onion until beginning to soften. If possible, transfer to the barbecue and fry until brown while the chicken is cooking. Or fry until brown and keep warm in a pan.

Lift the marinated slices of chicken out of the marinade and place on the greased grid. Barbecue for 10–12 minutes, turning once, until browned on the outside and cooked through when tested. Transfer the chicken tikka to a serving dish and top with the fried onions. Serve with plain boiled rice and the mint and cinnamon sauce. *Serves 4*

COCONUT CHICKEN WITH PEANUT SAUCE

8 chicken breast and wing portions
salt and freshly ground black pepper
1 teaspoon brown sugar

For the marinade:

1$\frac{1}{3}$ cups shredded coconut
1 tablespoon ground almonds
1 tablespoon ground ginger
1 teaspoon ground coriander
1 teaspoon ground turmeric

For the sauce:

2 medium-sized onions
1 cup roast salted peanuts
pinch of chili powder
3 tablespoons oil
$\frac{2}{3}$ cup water
1 teaspoon brown sugar
1 tablespoon soy sauce
1 tablespoon lemon juice
salt

First make the marinade. Pour 1$\frac{1}{4}$ cups boiling water over the coconut and leave for 30 minutes. Drain through a sieve, pressing the coconut. Mix together the almonds, ginger, coriander and turmeric, then gradually stir in the coconut milk.

126

Season the chicken portions with salt and pepper and place in a shallow dish. Pour over the marinade, cover and leave to stand for about 2 hours, turning the portions occasionally.

Meanwhile, make the sauce. Roughly chop one of the onions and place in a food processor or blender with the peanuts and chili powder. Blend until the ingredients are reduced to a paste.

Chop the remaining onion. Heat the oil in a pan and use to fry the chopped onion until soft and golden. Add the peanut paste and cook, stirring, for 3 minutes. Gradually blend in the water and sugar and cook for 5 minutes, stirring all the time. Mix in the soy sauce and lemon juice and season with salt to taste. Keep warm on the side of the barbecue.

Remove the chicken portions from the marinade, sprinkle with the sugar and arrange on the greased grid. Barbecue for about 50 minutes, turning and basting frequently with the marinade, until the outside is brown and crisp and juices run clear when tested. Serve with the warm sauce and lots of fluffy boiled rice. *Serves 8*

ORANGE GLAZED CHICKEN HALVES

4 (1–1¼-lb.) chicken halves
salt and freshly ground black pepper

For the marinade and glaze:

5 tablespoons clear honey
3 tablespoons lemon juice
finely grated rind of 1 orange
juice of 2 oranges
3 tablespoons Worcestershire sauce
1 tablespoon soy sauce

For the marinade and glaze, place all the ingredients in a pan and heat gently, stirring, for 2 minutes. Leave to cool.

Lay the chicken halves in a large shallow dish and season lightly with salt and pepper to taste. Pour over the marinade, cover and leave to stand for up to 24 hours, turning the chicken halves occasionally.

Lift out the chicken, reserving the marinade, and place in a roasting pan. Cook in a preheated moderate oven (350°F) for 1 hour.

When required, arrange the chicken halves on the grid and brush well with the reserved marinade. Barbecue for about 10 minutes, turning

frequently and brushing with more of the marinade, until well glazed and crisp. *Serves 4 generously*

TASTY DRUMSTICK PARCELS

8 chicken drumsticks
olive oil
8 zucchini
4 cloves of garlic, very finely chopped
1 teaspoon dried basil
2 teaspoons sugar
salt and freshly ground black pepper
1 tablespoon tomato paste

Have ready 8 squares of foil each large enough to enclose a drumstick and few slices of zucchini easily.

Brush the drumsticks all over with oil, place on the grid or under a hot broiler and cook for 2 minutes on each side. Top and tail the zucchini and cut into ½-inch slices.

Place each drumstick on a piece of foil, divide the zucchini slices among them and scatter over the garlic, basil and sugar and season with salt and pepper to taste. Top each drumstick with a little of the tomato paste and sprinkle lightly with oil. Fold up the foil and crimp the edges together to form airtight parcels.

Arrange the foil parcels on the grid. Barbecue for about 20 minutes, turning them over once during this time. Test one drumstick and if juices are at all pink, cook on for a further 2 minutes on each side and test again before serving. *Serves 8 or 4 generously if preferred*

INDEX

Apricot and bacon kebabs 76
Apricot and nut stuffed fruit bread 108
Apricot toppers, steaks with 104
Avocado dip, tangy 118

Bacon 34, 40:
 Apricot and bacon kebabs 76
 Bacon bites with spicy dip 71
 Bacon-stuffed eggplants 87
 Banana and bacon kebabs with
  curry sauce 76
 Onion smothered chops 48
Bananas with syrup and ginger 123
Barbecues:
 Foundations for 13
 Fuel and fire making for 20–1
 Improvised grills 11
 Types of manufactured 14–18
Beef 34, 40:
 Baked Indian kebabs 124
 Barbecued beef keftedes 64
 Beef brochettes with yogurt
  marinade 72
 Cheese and beef patties 119
 Harvest burgers 48
 Hot steakettes 58
 Mustard beef kebabs 70
 Relishburgers 44
 Rice and beefburgers 54
 Steak and kidney skewers 75
 Steaks with apricot toppers 104
 Steaks with hot sauce and
  barbecue fried rice 57
Beet slices, instant pickled 106
Bran rolls 108
Braziers 14
Broiling 32, 43–61
Built-in barbecues 12–13
Bulb baster 24
Butters:
 Basil and lemon butter 59
 Garlic and herb butter 104
 Orange and oregano butter 104
 Orange and tarragon butter 59
 Paprika and parsley butter 104

Campfire-style barbecue 12
Charcoal, charcoal briquets 20
Cheese ball, stuffed 115
Cheese and beef patties 119
Cheese and tuna pasta salad 116
Cheese and vegetable ring 115
Chicken 34, 40:
 Barbecue bean salad 96
 Blue cheese chicken 46
 Chicken and chive mustard kebabs
  75
 Chicken and mango kebabs with
  nut rice 68
 Chicken and pineapple kebabs 71
 Chicken with sweet and sour
  tomato sauce 54
 Chicken tikka with mint and
  cinnamon sauce 126
 Chinese chicken kebabs 67
 Coconut chicken with peanut sauce
  126
 Crispy chicken on sticks 68
 Curried chicken dip 118
 Devil's fiery drumsticks 60
 East Indian satay 76
 Herbed chicken 126
 Herby chicken fingers 44
 Honeyed chicken breasts 58
 Malayan curried chicken 120
 Molasses basted chicken
  drumsticks 58
 Moroccan rotisserie chicken 82
 Orange glazed chicken halves 127
 Tandoori chicken 124
 Tasty drumstick parcels 127
Chocolate dip, rich 110
Chocolate fudge cake, chilled 119
Chutney 107
Citronella candles 26

Cleaning-up equipment 26
Cod:
 Otak otak 88
Concertina cooking 33
Corn chutney 107
Corn in the husk, barbecued 108
Corn and pineapple parcels 87
Crab-stuffed turkey breasts 86
Cranberry dip, spiced 115
Cranberry orange spareribs 54

Dips:
 Butterscotch dip 110
 Chili and ham dip 118
 Corn and pepper dip 115
 Curried chicken dip 118
 Curry cheese dip 115
 Rich chocolate dip 110
 Sour cream and peanut dip 76
 Spiced cranberry dip 115
 Tangy avocado dip 118
Duck, duckling 34, 40:
 Honeyed duck portions 58
 Spiced orange duckling portions 123
 Spit-roast ducklings with apricot
  glaze 85

Eggplants, bacon-stuffed 87
Electric barbecues 18

Fish 34, 35–6. See also Mackerel etc.
 Barbecued fish kebabs 78
 Fish teriyaki 89
Frankfurters, spicy 58
Fruit 41. See also Apricot etc.
 Barbecued fruit salad 110

Garden pickle, colorful 106
Gas barbecues 17–18
Goulash soup 116

Ham 34, 40:
 Chili and ham dip 118
 Ham and cheese stuffed potatoes
  116
 Ham with peach cups 57
 Smoked slices with cherry
  barbecue sauce 44
 Mustardy ham kebabs 78
 Roquefort-topped ham slices 50
 Waikiki kebabs 72
Hamburgers 40
Hibachis 16
Hickory chips 24

Kebab and skewer cooking 32, 63–79,
 124
Kettle barbecues 14–15
Kidney:
 Lamb and kidney kebabs 71
 Pickled onion kebabs 72
 Saucy liver and kidney kebabs 74
 Sausage and kidney kebabs 64
 Steak and kidney skewers 75

Lamb 34, 40:
 Baked Indian kebabs 124
 Butterflied leg of lamb 57
 Farm burgers 50
 Fruity tandoori lamb skewers 70
 Lamb chops with minted onion
  sauce 116
 Lamb chops with rich apple sauce
  52
 Lamb and kidney kebabs 71
 Lamb and peanut burgers 50
 Lamb skewers with rosemary 68
 Lamb steaks with fruit side dish 85
 Lamb and tarragon mustard kebabs
  75
 Rice and lamb burgers 54
 Spit-roast lamb with beans 82
 Wanaka barbecued lamb spareribs
  75
 Wellington lamb kebabs 74

Lettuce treasures 120
Liver and kidney kebabs 74

Mackerel, mustardy 55
Marshmallows, toasted 114
Meat 40. See also Beef etc.
 Mixed barbecue meats with three
  dips 118
 Three harmony satay 120
Meat thermometer 26
Mixed broil with marmalade glaze 59
Mullet:
 Beach barbecued mullet or snapper
  59
 Italian fish bake 88
Mushrooms, marinated, with herb
 stuffing 104

Onion smothered bacon slices 48
Oranges, gingered 123
Otak otak 88

Parcel cooking 30, 86–9
Pastry twists 108
Peas, French 87
Pickles 106
Pineapple:
 Celestial pineapple 121
 Chicken and pineapple kebabs 71
 Peppery pineapple 115
 Pork steaks with pineapple crowns 57
 Spicy pork and fresh pineapple
  kebabs 67
 Syrupy pineapple with coconut 123
Pit-cooking 19
Pizzas, quick French bread 119
Pork 34, 40:
 Apple mustard pork kebabs 70
 Cranberry orange spareribs 54
 Crunchy pork strips 44
 Easy barbecued spareribs 61
 Farm burgers 50
 Pork chops provençale 52
 Pork kebabs with pita pockets 75
 Pork rib chops with tomato pepper
  sauce 61
 Pork steaks with pineapple crowns 57
 Rice and pork burgers 54
 Spareribs with sweet and sour
  tomato sauce 60
 Spicy pork and fresh pineapple
  kebabs 67
 Sweet and sour spareribs 60
Portable barbecues 17
Potato:
 Baked potato skin toppings 107
 Barbecued potato slices 104
 Ham and cheese stuffed potatoes
  116
 Paprika potato slices 104
Poultry 40. See also Chicken etc.

Rice:
 Barbecue fried rice 57
 Brown rice salad 96
 Fruity rice and mustard salad 96
 Mixed vegetable pilaff 124
 Nut rice 68
 Rice and beef burgers 54
 Walnut rice salad 96

Salads:
 Barbecue bean salad 96
 Barbecued fruit salad 110
 Bean and smoked mackerel salad 96
 Brown rice salad 96
 Carrot and raisin salad 99
 Cauliflower summer salad 96
 Chinese orange salad 95
 Dressed bean and onion salad 92
 Fennel and orange salad 95
 Fruity rice and mustard salad 96
 Grapefruit and avocado cups 98
 Green and white dressed salad 123
 Indian side salad 125

Italian mushroom salad 96
Lettuce, orange and almond salad 95
Melon and shrimp salad 99
Oriental pasta salad 97
Prawn or shrimp and pasta salad 95
Radicchio and pineapple pasta
 salad 92
Summer orange and rose salad 110
Tuna and pepper rice 92
Tuna salad royale 98
Walnut rice salad 96
Salmon:
 Lime basted salmon steaks 88
 Salmon, mushroom and marjoram
  parcels 59
 Salmon with orange and tarragon
  butter 59
 Salmon steaks with basil and
  lemon butter 59
 Salmon steaks with flambéed
  pineapple 88
 Simple barbecued salmon steaks 88
Sauces and dressings:
 Apple sauce 52
 Caribbean cream dressing 100
 Curry sauce 76, 99
 Fresh herb sauce 50
 Herby red wine marinade 100
 Hot sauce 57
 Mint and cinnamon sauce 126
 Mint and yogurt marinade 100
 Peanut and mushroom sauce 64
 Peanut sauce 126
 Pimento yogurt dressing 100
 Red currant sweet and sour sauce 99
 South Sea sauce 50
 Spiced red plum sauce 100
 Sweet and sour tomato sauce 60
 Turkish yogurt dressing 100
Sausage links 34, 40:
 Rice and sausage burgers 54
 Sausage and kidney kebabs 64
 Skewered sausage meatballs 66
 Skewered sausages 78
 Spicy frankfurters 58
 Spicy sausages 58
Searing 33
Skewer and kebab cooking 32, 63–79
Spit-roasting 32, 81–5; – rod 24

Tandoori chicken 124
Tomato and cucumber chutney 107
Tomatoes, herby stuffed 123
Tool set 23
Trout in newspaper and variations 36
Tuna:
 Cheese and tuna pasta salad 116
 Tuna and pepper rice 92
 Tuna salad royale 98
Turkey 34, 40:
 Cider and turkey soup 114
 Crab-stuffed turkey breasts 86
 Honeyed turkey fillets 58
 Kettle-roast turkey 85
 Ribboned turkey sausages with
  dips 114
 Spit-roast gingered turkey roll 82
 Spit-roast turkey with spiced apple 85
 Turkey fillets with cherry barbecue
  sauce 44
 Turkey kebabs with beer baste 114

Universal barbecue 18

Variety meats 40
Vegetables 40–1. See also Eggplant
 etc.
 Curried vegetable and nut burgers 47
 Mixed vegetable pilaff 124
 Vegetable kebabs with peanut and
  mushroom sauce 64

Wagons 15–16; gas 18
Walnut rice salad 96
Wire broilers 24